Sir Edward Bulwer Lytton

The Dramatic Works

Volume I.

Sir Edward Bulwer Lytton

The Dramatic Works
Volume I.

ISBN/EAN: 9783742825568

Manufactured in Europe, USA, Canada, Australia, Japa

Cover: Foto ©Andreas Hilbeck / pixelio.de

Manufactured and distributed by brebook publishing software (www.brebook.com)

Sir Edward Bulwer Lytton

The Dramatic Works

COLLECTION
OF
BRITISH AUTHORS.
VOL. 531.

THE DRAMATIC WORKS
OF
SIR EDWARD BULWER LYTTON, BART.

IN TWO VOLUMES.

VOL. I.

TAUCHNITZ EDITION.
By the same Author,

PELHAM, or the adventures of a gentleman (w. portrait) . 1 v.
EUGENE ARAM . . . . 1 v.
PAUL CLIFFORD . . . . 1 v.
ZANONI . . . . 1 v.
THE LAST DAYS OF POMPEII . . . . 1 v.
THE DISOWNED . . . . 1 v.
ERNEST MALTRAVERS . . . . 1 v.
ALICE, or the mysteries . . . . 1 v.
EVA AND THE PILGRIMS OF THE RHINE . . . . . 1 v.
DEVEREUX . . . . 1 v.
GODOLPHIN AND FALKLAND . . . . 1 v.
RIENZI, the last of the Roman tribunes . . . . 1 v.
NIGHT AND MORNING . . . . 1 v.
THE LAST OF THE BARONS . . . . 2 v.
ATHENS, its rise and fall . . . . 2 v.
THE POEMS AND BALLADS OF SCHILLER . . . . . 1 v.
LUCRETIA, or the children of night . . . . 2 v.
HAROLD, the last of the Saxon kings . . . . 2 v.
KING ARTHUR, a poem . . . . 2 v.
THE NEW TIMON AND ST STEPHEN'S . . . . 1 v.
THE CAXTONS, a family picture . . . . 2 v.
MY NOVEL, or varieties in English life . . . . . . 4 v.
WHAT WILL HE DO WITH IT? . . . . 4 v.
A STRANGE STORY . . . . 2 v.
CAXTONIANA . . . . 2 v.
THE LOST TALES OF MILETUS . . . . 1 v.
MISCELLANEOUS PROSE WORKS . . . . 4 v.
THE ODES AND EPODES OF HORACE . . . . 2 v.

THE
DRAMATIC WORKS

OF

SIR EDWARD BULWER LYTTON, Bart.

COPYRIGHT EDITION.

IN TWO VOLUMES.

VOL. I.

RICHELIEU.—MONEY.

LEIPZIG

BERNHARD TAUCHNITZ

1860.

RICHELIEU;

OR,

THE CONSPIRACY.

"Le Comte de Soissons, et le Duc de Bouillon, avaient une bonne armée, et ils savaient la conduire; et pour plus grande sûreté, tandis que cette armée devait s'avancer, on devait assassiner le Cardinal et faire soulever Paris... Les Conjurés faisaient un traité avec l'Espagne pour introduire des troupes en France, et pour y mettre tout en confusion dans une Régence qu'on croyait prochaine, et dont chacun espérait profiter... Richelieu avait perdu toute sa faveur, et ne conservait que l'avantage d'être nécessaire. Le bonheur du Cardinal voulut encore que le complot fut découvert, et qu'une copie du traité lui tombât entre les mains." — *Voltaire, Hist. Gén.*

PREFACE.

The administration of Cardinal Richelieu, whom (despite all his darker qualities) Voltaire and history justly consider the true architect of the French monarchy, and the great parent of French civilization, is characterised by features alike tragic and comic. A weak king — an ambitious favourite; a despicable conspiracy against the minister, nearly always associated with a dangerous treason against the State — these, with little variety of names and dates, constitute the eventful cycle through which, with a dazzling ease, and an arrogant confidence, the great luminary fulfilled its destinies. Blent together, in startling contrast, we see the grandest achievements and the pettiest agents; — the spy — the mistress — the capuchin; — the destruction of feudalism; — the humiliation of Austria; — the dismemberment of Spain.

Richelieu himself is still what he was in his own day — a man of two characters. If, on the one hand, he is justly represented as inflexible and vindictive, crafty and unscrupulous; so, on the other, it cannot be denied that he was placed in times in which the long impunity of every license required stern examples — that he was beset by perils and intrigues, which gave a certain excuse to the subtlest inventions of self-defence — that his ambition was inseparably connected with a passionate love for the glory of his country — and that, if he was her dictator, he was not less her benefactor. It has been fairly remarked, by the most impartial historians, that he was no less generous to merit than severe to crime — that, in the various departments of the State, the Army, and the Church, he selected and distinguished the ablest aspirants — that the wars which he conducted were, for the most part, essential to the preservation of France, and Europe itself, from the formidable encroachments of the Austrian House — that, in spite of those wars, the people were not oppressed with exorbitant imposts — and that he left the kingdom he had governed in a more flourishing and vigorous state than at any former period of the French history, or at the decease of Louis XIV.

The cabals formed against this great statesman were not carried on by the patriotism of public virtue, or the emulation of equal talent: they were but court struggles, in which the most worthless agents had recourse to the most desperate means. In each, as I have before observed, we see combined the twofold attempt to murder the minister and to betray the country. Such, then, are the agents, and such the designs with which truth, in the drama as in history, requires us to contrast the celebrated Cardinal; — not disguising his foibles or his vices, but not unjust to the grander qualities (especially the love of country), by which they were often dignified, and, at times, redeemed.

The historical drama is the concentration of historical events. In the attempt to place upon the stage the picture of an era, that license with dates and details, which Poetry permits, and which the highest authorities in the Drama of France herself have sanctioned, has

PREFACE. 5

been, though not unsparingly, indulged. The conspiracy of the Duc de Bouillon is, for instance, amalgamated with the *denouement* of *The Day of Dupes*;* and circumstances connected with the treason of Cinq Mars (whose brilliant youth and gloomy catastrophe tend to subvert poetic and historic justice, by seducing us to forget his base ingratitude, and his perfidious apostasy) are identified with the fate of the earlier favourite Baradas,** whose sudden rise and as sudden fall passed into a proverb. I ought to add, that the noble romance of "Cinq Mars" suggested one of the scenes in the fifth act; and that for the conception of some portion of the intrigue connected with De Mauprat and Julie, I am, with great alterations of incident, and considerable if not entire reconstruction of character, indebted to an early and admirable novel by the author of "Picciola."***

LONDON, *March* 1839.

---

* "Le Cardinal se croit perdu, et prépare sa retraite. Ses amis lui conseillent de tenter enfin auprès du Roi un nouvel effort. Le Cardinal va trouver le Roi à Versailles. Le Roi, qui avait sacrifié son ministre par faiblesse, se remit par faiblesse entre ses mains, et il lui abandonne ceux qui l'avaient perdu. Ce jour qui est encore à présent appellé *La Journée des Dupes*, fut celui du pouvoir absolu du Cardinal." — *Voltaire, Hist. Gen.*

** "En six mois il (le Roi) fit (Baradas) premier Ecuyer, premier Gentilhomme de la Chambre, Capitaine de St. Germain, et Lieutenant de Roi, en Champagne. En moins de temps encore, on lui ôta tout, et des débris de sa grandeur, à peine lui resta-t-il de quoi payer ses dettes: de sorte que pour signifier une grande fortune dissipée aussi qu'acquise on disait en commun proverbe, *Fortune de Baradas.*" — *Anquetil.*

*** It may be as well, however, to caution the English reader against some of the impressions which the eloquence of both the writers I refer to are calculated to leave. They have exaggerated the more evil, and have kept out of sight the nobler qualities of the Cardinal.

NOTE.

The length of the play necessarily requires curtailments on the stage — the principal of which are enclosed within brackets. Many of the passages thus omitted, however immaterial to the audience, must obviously be such as the *reader* would be least inclined to dispense with — viz., those which, without being absolutely essential to the business of the stage, contain either the subtler strokes of character, or the more poetical embellishments of description. An important consequence of these suppressions is, that Richelieu himself is left, too often and too unrelievedly, to positions which place him in an *amiable* light, without that shadowing forth of his more sinister motives and his fiercer qualities, which is attempted in the written play. Thus, the *character* takes a degree of credit due only to the *situation*. To judge the author's conception of Richelieu fairly, and to estimate how far it is consistent with historical portraiture, the play must be *read*.

TO

THE MARQUIS OF LANSDOWNE, K.G.,

&c., &c.,

THIS DRAMA

IS INSCRIBED,

IN TRIBUTE TO THE TALENTS WHICH COMMAND, AND THE QUALITIES WHICH ENDEAR, RESPECT.

DRAMATIS PERSONÆ

LOUIS THE THIRTEENTH.
GASTON, DUKE OF ORLEANS, *brother to Louis XIII.*
BARADAS, *favourite of the King, First Gentleman of the Chamber, Premier Ecuyer, &c.*
CARDINAL RICHELIEU.
THE CHEVALIER DE MAUPRAT.
THE SIEUR DE BERINGHEN, *in attendance on the King,* [*] *one of the Conspirators.*
JOSEPH, *a Capuchin, Richelieu's confidant.*
HUGUET, *an officer of Richelieu's household guard — a Spy.*
FRANÇOIS, *First Page to Richelieu.*
FIRST COURTIER.
CAPTAIN OF THE ARCHERS.
FIRST, SECOND, THIRD SECRETARIES OF STATE.
GOVERNOR OF THE BASTILE.
GAOLER.

Courtiers, Pages, Conspirators, Officers, Soldiers, &c.

JULIE DE MORTEMAR, *an Orphan, ward to Richelieu.*
MARION DE LORME, *Mistress to Orleans, but in Richelieu's pay.*

[*] Properly speaking, the King's First Valet de Chambre — a post of great importance at that time.

RICHELIEU;
OR,
THE CONSPIRACY.

ACT I.

FIRST DAY.

SCENE I. — *A room in the house of* MARION DE LORME; *a table towards the front of the stage (with wine, fruits, &c), at which are seated* BARADAS, *Four Courtiers, splendidly dressed in the costume of* 1641-2; — *the* DUKE OF ORLEANS *reclining on a large fauteuil;* — MARION DE LORME *standing at the back of his chair, offers him a goblet, and then retires. At another table*, DE BERINGHEN, DE MAUPRAT, *playing at dice; other Courtiers, of inferior rank to those at the table of the Duke, looking on.*

 Orle. [*drinking*]. Here's to our enterprise!
 Bar. [*glancing at* MARION]. Hush, sir!
 Orle. [*aside*].   Nay, Count,
You may trust her; she doats on me; no house
So safe as Marion's. *[At our statelier homes
The very walls do play the eaves-dropper.
There's not a sunbeam creeping o'er our floors
But seems a glance from that malignant eye
Which reigns o'er France; our fatal greatness lives
In the sharp glare of one relentless day.

 * The passages enclosed in brackets are omitted in representation.

But Richelieu's self forgets to fear the sword
The myrtle hides; and Marion's silken robe
Casts its kind charity o'er fiercer sins
Than those which haunt the rosy path between
The lip and eye of beauty. — Oh, no house
So safe as Marion's.]
  Bar.   Still, we have a secret.
And oil and water — woman and a secret —
Are hostile properties.
  Orle.   Well — Marion, see
How the play prospers yonder.
    [Marion *goes to the next table, looks on for a few moments, then exit.*
  Bar. [*producing a parchment*]. I have now
All the conditions drawn; it only needs
Our signatures: upon receipt of this,
(Whereto is join'd the schedule of our treaty
With the Count-Duke,* the Richelieu of the Escurial,)
Bouillon will join his army with the Spaniard,
March on to Paris, — there, dethrone the King:
You will be Regent; I, and ye, my Lords,
Form the new Council. So much for the core
Of our great scheme.
  Orle.   But Richelieu is an Argus;
One of his hundred eyes will light upon us,
And then — good-bye to life.
  Bar.   To gain the prize
We must destroy the Argus: — ay, my Lords,

---

* Olivares, Minister of Spain.

The scroll the core, but blood must fill the veins,
Of our design; — while this despatch'd to Bouillon,
Richelieu despatch'd to heaven! — The last *my* charge.
Meet here to-morrow night. *You*, sir, as first
In honour and in hope, meanwhile select
Some trusty knave to bear the scroll to Bouillon;
Midst Richelieu's foes *I'll* find some desperate hand
To strike for vengeance, while we stride to power.

 Orle. So be it; — to-morrow, midnight. Come, my
  Lords.

  [*Exeunt* ORLEANS, *and the* Courtiers *in his train. Those
  at the other table rise, salute* ORLEANS, *and reseat
  themselves.*

 De Ber. Double the stakes.
 De Mau.   Done.
 De Ber.   Bravo; faith, it shames me
To bleed a purse already *in extremis.*

 De Mau. Nay, as you've had the patient to yourself
So long, no other doctor should despatch it.

      [DE MAUPRAT *throws and loses.*

 Omnes. Lost! Ha, ha! — poor De Mauprat!
 De Ber.   One throw more?
 De Mau. No; I am bankrupt [*pushing gold*]. There
  goes all — except
My honour and my sword.   [*They rise.*
 De Ber.   Long cloaks and honour
Went out of vogue together, when we found
We got on much more rapidly without them;
The sword, indeed, is never out of fashion, —
The devil has care of *that.*

First Gamester.   Ay, take the sword
To Cardinal Richelieu: — he gives gold for steel,.
When worn by brave men.
    De Mau.   Richelieu!
    De Ber. [*to* BARADAS],   At that name
He changes colour, bites his nether lip.
Ev'n in his brightest moments whisper "Richelieu,"
And you cloud all his sunshine.
    Bar.   I have mark'd it,·
And I will learn the wherefore.
    De Mau.   The Egyptian
Dissolved her richest jewel in a draught:
Would I could so melt time and all its treasures,
And drain it thus.   [*Drinking.*
    De Ber.   Come, gentlemen, what say ye,
A walk on the parade?
    Omnes.   Ay; come, De Mauprat.
    De Mau. Pardon me; we shall meet again ere nightfall.
    Bar. I'll stay and comfort Mauprat.
    De Ber.   Comfort! — when
We gallant fellows have run out a friend,
There's nothing left — except to run him through!
There's the last act of friendship.
    De Mau.   Let me keep
That favour in reserve; in all beside
Your most obedient servant.
        [*Exeunt* DE BERINGHEN, *&c. Manent* DE MAUPRAT
            and BARADAS.
    Bar.   You have lost —
You are not sad.

De Mau.   Sad! — Life and gold have wings,
And must fly one day: — open, then, their cages
And wish them merry.
　　Bar.　　　　You're a strange enigma: —
Fiery in war — and yet to glory lukewarm;
All mirth in action — in repose all gloom —
These are extremes in which the unconscious heart
Betrays the fever of deep-fix'd disease.
Confide in me! our young days roll'd together
In the same river, glassing the same stars
That smile i' the heaven of hope; — alike we made
Bright-winged steeds of our unform'd chimeras,
Spurring the fancies upward to the air,
Wherein we shaped fair castles from the cloud.
Fortune of late has sever'd us — and led
Me to the rank of Courtier, Count and Favourite, —
You to the titles of the wildest gallant
And bravest knight in France; — are you content?
No; — trust in me — some gloomy secret —
　　De Mau.　　　　　　　　　　Ay: —
A secret that doth haunt me, as, of old,
Men were possess'd of fiends! — Where'er I turn,
The grave yawns dark before me! — I *will* trust you; —
Hating the Cardinal, and beguiled by Orleans,
You know I join'd the Languedoc revolt —
Was captured — sent to the Bastile —
　　Bar.　　　　　　　　　　　But shared
The general pardon, which the Duke of Orleans
Won for himself and all in the revolt,
Who but obey'd his orders.

De Mau. Note the phrase; —
"*Obey'd his orders.*" Well, when on my way
To join the duke in Languedoc, I (then
The down upon my lip — less man than boy)
Leading young valours — reckless as myself,
Seized on the town of Faviaux, and displaced
The royal banners for the rebel Orleans
(Never too daring,) when I reach'd the camp,
Blamed me for acting — mark — *without his orders:*
Upon this quibble Richelieu razed my name
Out of the general pardon.
 Bar.   Yet released you
From the Bastile —
 De Mau.   To call me to his presence,
And thus address me: — "You have seized a town
Of France, without the orders of your leader,
And for this treason, but one sentence — DEATH."
 Bar. Death!
 De Mau. "I have pity on your youth and birth,
Nor wish to glut the headsman; — join your troop,
Now on the march against the Spaniards; — change
The traitor's scaffold for the soldier's grave; —
Your memory stainless — they who shared your crime
Exiled or dead — your king shall never learn it."
 Bar. O tender pity! — O most charming prospect!
Blown into atoms by a bomb, or drill'd
Into a cullender by gunshot! — Well? —
 De Mau. You have heard if I fought bravely. —
   Death became
Desired as Daphne by the eager Daygod.

Like him I chased the nymph — to grasp the laurel!
I could not die!
    Bar.   Poor fellow!
    De Mau.   When the Cardinal
Review'd the troops — his eye met mine; — he frown'd,
Summon'd me forth — "How's this!" quoth he; "you
      have shunn'd
The sword — beware the axe! — 'twill fall one day!"
He left me thus — we were recall'd to Paris,
And — you know all!
    Bar.   And, knowing this, why halt you,
Spell'd by the rattle-snake, — while in the breasts
Of your firm friends beat hearts, that vow the death
Of your grim tyrant? — Wake! — Be one of us;
The time invites — the king detests the Cardinal,
Dares not disgrace — but groans to be deliver'd
Of that too great a subject — join your friends,
Free France, and save yourself.
    De Mau.   Hush! Richelieu bears
A charmèd life; — to all, who have braved his power,
One common end — the block.
    Bar.   Nay, if he live,
The block your doom: —
    De Mau.   Better the victim, Count,
Than the assassin. — France requires a Richelieu,
But does not need a Mauprat. Truce to this; —
All time one midnight, where my thoughts are
      spectres.
What to my fame? — What love? —
    Bar.   Yet dost thou love *not?*

De Mau. Love? — I am young —
Bar. And Julie fair! [*Aside.*] It is so,
Upon the margin of the grave — his hand
Would pluck the rose that I would win and wear!
[*Aloud.*] — [Thou lov'st —
De Mau. Who, lonely in the midnight tent,
Gazed on the watch-fires in the sleepless air,
Nor chose one star amidst the clustering hosts
To bless it in the name of some fair face
Set in his spirit, as that star in Heaven?
For our divine affections, like the spheres
Move ever, over musical.
Bar. You speak
As one who fed on poetry.
De Mau. Why, man,
The thoughts of lovers stir with poetry
As leaves with summer-wind. — The heart that loves
Dwells in an Eden, hearing angel-lutes,
As Eve in the First Garden. Hast thou seen
My Julie, and not felt it henceforth dull
To live in the common world — and talk in words
That clothe the feelings of the frigid herd? —
Upon the perfumed pillow of her lips —
As on his native bed of roses flushed
With Paphian skies — Love smiling sleeps: — Her
    voice
The blest interpreter of thoughts as pure
As virgin wells where Dian takes delight,
Or fairies dip their changelings! — In the maze
Of her harmonious beauties — Modesty

(Like some severer grace that leads the choir
Of her sweet sisters) every airy motion
Attunes to such chaste charm, that Passion holds
His burning breath, and will not with a sigh
Dissolve the spell that binds him! — Oh those eyes
That woo the earth — shadowing more soul than lurks
Under the lids of Psyche! — Go! — thy lip
Curls at the purfled phrases of a lover —
Love thou, and if thy love be deep as mine,
Thou wilt not laugh at poets.
    Bar. [*aside*].   With each word
Thou wak'st a jealous demon in my heart,
And my hand clutches at my hilt. —]
    De Mau. [*gaily*].   No more! —
I love! — Your breast holds both my secrets! — Never
Unbury either! — Come, while yet we may,
We'll bask us in the noon of rosy life: —
Lounge through the gardens, — flaunt it in the taverns, —
Laugh, — game, — drink, — feast: — If so confined
      my days,
Faith, I'll enclose the nights — Pshaw! not so grave;
I'm a true Frenchman! — *Vive la bagatelle!*

    [*As they are going out, enter* HUGUET *and four* Arquebusiers.

    Hug. Messire De Mauprat, — I arrest you! — Follow
To the Lord Cardinal.
    De Mau.   You see, my friend,
I'm out of my suspense! — the tiger's play'd
Long enough with his prey. — Farewell! — Hereafter

Say, when men name me, "Adrien de Mauprat
Lived without hope, and perish'd without fear!"
      [*Exeunt* DE MAUPRAT, HUGUET, *&c.*
 Bar. Farewell! — I trust for ever! I design'd thee
For Richelieu's murderer — but, as well his martyr!
In childhood you the stronger — and I cursed you;
In youth the fairer — and I cursed you still;
And now my rival! — While the name of Julie
Hung on thy lips — I smiled — for then I saw,
In my mind's eye, the cold and grinning Death
Hang o'er thy head the pall! — Ambition, Love,
Ye twin-born stars of daring destinies,
Sit in my house of Life! — By the king's aid
I will be Julie's husband — in despite
Of my Lord Cardinal! — by the king's aid
I will be minister of France — in spite
Of my Lord Cardinal! — And then — what then?
The king loves Julie — feeble prince — false master —
    [*Producing and gazing on the parchment.*
Then, by the aid of Bouillon, and the Spaniard,
I will dethrone the king; and all — ha! — ha! —
All, in despite of my Lord Cardinal!   [*Exit.*

SCENE II.

A room in the Palais Cardinal, the walls hung with arras. A large screen in one corner. A table covered with books, papers, &c. A rude clock in a recess. Busts, statues, bookcases, weapons of different periods and banners suspended over RICHELIEU's *chair.*

RICHELIEU *and* JOSEPH.

Rich. And so you think this new conspiracy
The craftiest trap yet laid for the old fox? —
Fox! — Well, I like the nickname! What did Plutarch
Say of the Greek Lysander?
 Joseph.   I forget.
 Rich. That where the lion's skin fell short, he
  eked it
Out with the fox's! A great statesman, Joseph,
That same Lysander!
 Joseph.   Orleans heads the traitors.
 Rich. A very wooden head, then! Well?
 Joseph.   The favourite,
Count Baradas —
 Rich.   A weed of hasty growth;
First gentleman of the chamber — titles, lands,
And the king's ear! — It cost me six long winters
To mount as high, as in six little moons
This painted lizard — But I hold the ladder,
And when I shake — he falls! What more?
 Joseph.   A scheme
To make your orphan-ward an instrument

To aid your foes. You placed her with the queen,
One of the royal chamber, — as a watch
I' th' enemy's quarters —
    Rich.   And the silly child
Visits me daily, — calls me "Father," — prays
Kind Heaven to bless me — And for all the rest
As well have placed a doll about the queen!
She does not heed who frowns — who smiles; with
    whom
The king confers in whispers; notes not when
Men who last week were foes, are found in corners
Mysteriously affectionate; words spoken
Within closed doors she never hears; — by chance
Taking the air at keyholes — Senseless puppet!
No ears — nor eyes! — and yet she says, "She loves
    me!"
Go on —
    Joseph. Your ward has charm'd the king —
    Rich.   Out on you!
Have I not, one by one, from such fair shoots
Pluck'd the insidious ivy of his love?
And shall it creep around my blossoming tree
Where innocent thoughts, like happy birds, make music
That spirits in Heaven might hear? They're sinful, too,
Those passionate surfeits of the rampant flesh,
The church condemns them; and to us, my Joseph,
The props and pillars of the church, most hurtful.
The king is weak — whoever the king loves
Must rule the king; the lady loves another,
The other rules the lady — thus we're balk'd

Of our own proper sway — The king must have
No goddess but the State: — the State — that's
    Richelieu!
    Joseph. This not the worst; — Louis, in all decorous,
And deeming you her least compliant guardian,
Would veil his suit by marriage with his minion,
Your prosperous foe, Count Baradas!
    Rich.   Ha! ha!
I have another bride for Baradas.
    Joseph. You, my lord?
    Rich.   Ay — more faithful than the love
Of fickle woman: — when the head lies lowliest,
Clasping him fondest; — Sorrow never knew.
So sure a soother, — and her bed is stainless!
    Joseph [*aside*]. If of the grave he speaks, I do not
        wonder
That priests are bachelors!

                Enter FRANÇOIS.

    Fran.   Mademoiselle de Mortemar.
    Rich. Most opportune — admit her. [*Exit* FRANÇOIS.
                                In my closet
You'll find a rosary, Joseph; ere you tell
Three hundred beads, I'll summon you. Stay, Joseph; —
I did omit an Ave in my matins, —
A grievous fault; — atone it for me, Joseph;
There is a scourge within; I am weak, you strong.
It were but charity to take my sin
On such broad shoulders. Exercise is healthful.
    Joseph. I! guilty of such criminal presumption

As to mistake myself for you — No, never!
Think it not! [*Aside.*] Troth, a pleasant invitation!
           [*Exit* JOSEPH.

   Enter JULIE DE MORTEMAR.

 Rich. That's my sweet Julie! — why, upon this face
Blushes such daybreak, one might swear the morning
Were come to visit Tithon.
 Julie [*placing herself at his feet*]. Are you gracious? —
May I say "Father?"
 Rich.   Now and ever!
 Julie.   Father!
A sweet word to an orphan.
 Rich.   No; not orphan
While Richelieu lives; thy father loved me well;
My friend, ere I had flatterers (now, I'm great,
In other phrase, I'm friendless) — he died young
In years, not service, and bequeath'd thee to me;
And thou shalt have a dowry, girl, to buy
Thy mate amidst the mightiest. Drooping? — sighs?
Art thou not happy at the court?
 Julie.   Not often.
 Rich. [*aside*]. Can she love Baradas? Ah! at thy heart
There's what can smile and sigh, blush and grow pale,
All in a breath? Thou art admired — art young;
Does not his majesty commend thy beauty —
Ask thee to sing to him? — and swear such sounds
Had smooth'd the brows of Saul?

Julie. He's very tiresome,
Our worthy king.
    Rich. Fie! kings are never tiresome,
Save to their ministers. What courtly gallants
Charm ladies most? — De Sourdiac, Longueville, or
The favourite Baradas?
    Julie. A smileless man —
I fear and shun him.
    Rich. Yet he courts thee?
    Julie. Then
He is more tiresome than his Majesty.
    Rich. Right, girl, shun Baradas. Yet of these
      flowers
Of France, not one, in whose more honied breath
Thy heart hears summer whisper?
        Enter HUGUET.
    Hug. The Chevalier
De Mauprat waits below.
    Julie [*starting up*]. De Mauprat!
    Rich. Hem!
He has been tiresome too! — Anon. [*Exit* HUGUET.
    Julie. What doth he? —
I mean — I — Does your Eminence — that is —
Know you Messire de Mauprat?
    Rich. Well! — and you —
Has he address'd you often?
    Julie. Often! — No —
Nine times; — nay, ten; the last time, by the lattice
Of the great staircase. [*In a melancholy tone.*] The
    Court sees him rarely.

Rich. A bold and forward royster!
Julie. He? nay, modest,
Gentle, and sad, methinks.
Rich. Wears gold and azure?
Julie. No; sable.
Rich. So you note his colours, Julie?
Shame on you, child; look loftier. By the mass,
I have business with this modest gentleman.
 Julie. You're angry with poor Julie. There's no
  cause.
 Rich. No cause — you hate my foes?
 Julie. I do!
 Rich. Hate Mauprat?
 Julie. Not Mauprat. No, not Adrien, father.
 Rich. Adrien!
Familiar! — Go, child; no, not *that* way; wait
In the tapestry chamber; I will join you, — go.
 Julie. His brows are knit; I dare not call him father!
But I *must* speak — Your Eminence —
 Rich. [*sternly*]. Well, girl!
 Julie. Nay,
Smile on me — one smile more; there, now I'm happy.
Do not rank Mauprat with your foes; he is not,
I know he *is* not; he loves France too well.
 Rich. Not rank De Mauprat with my foes? So be it.
I'll blot him from that list.
 Julie. That's my own father.
            [*Exit* JULIE.
 Rich. [*ringing a small bell on the table*]. Huguet!

Enter HUGUET.

De Mauprat struggled not, nor murmured?

Hug. No; proud and passive.

Rich. Bid him enter. — Hold:
Look that he hide no weapon. Humph, despair
Makes victims sometimes victors. When he has enter'd
Glide round unseen; — place thyself yonder [*pointing
    to the screen*]; watch him;
If he show violence — (let me see thy carbine;
So, a good weapon;) — if he play the lion,
Why — the dog's death.

Hug. I never miss my mark.

    [*Exit* HUGUET; RICHELIEU *seats himself at the table, and
    slowly arranges the papers before him. Enter* DE
    MAUPRAT, *preceded by* HUGUET, *who then retires
    behind the screen.*

Rich. Approach, sir. — Can you call to mind the hour,
Now three years since, when in this room, methinks,
Your presence honour'd me?

De Mau. It is, my Lord,
One of my most —

Rich. [*drily*]. Delightful recollections.*

De Mau. [*aside*]. St. Denis! doth he make a jest of axe
And headsman?

---

  * There are many anecdotes of the irony, often so terrible, in which Richelieu indulged. But he had a love for humour in its more hearty and genial shape. He would send for Boisrobert "to make him laugh," — and grave ministers and magnates waited in the ante-room, while the great cardinal listened and responded to the sallies of the lively wit.

Rich. [*sternly*]. I did then accord you
A mercy ill requited — you still live?
De Mau. To meet death face to face at last.
Rich.   Your words
Are bold.
De Mau. My deeds have not belied them.
Rich.   Deeds!
O miserable delusion of man's pride!
Deeds! cities sack'd, fields ravaged, hearths profaned,
Men butcher'd! In your hour of doom behold
The *deeds* you boast of! From rank showers of blood,
And the red light of blazing roofs, you build
The rainbow glory, and to shuddering conscience
Cry, — Lo, the bridge to Heaven!
De Mau.   If war be sinful,
Your hand the gauntlet cast.
Rich.   It was so, sir.
Note the distinction: — I weigh'd well the cause
Which made the standard holy; raised the war
But to secure the peace. Franco bled — I groan'd;
But look'd beyond; and, in the vista, saw
France saved, and I exulted. You — but you
Were but the tool of slaughter — knowing nought,
Foreseeing nought, nought hoping, nought lamenting,
And for nought fit — save cutting throats for hire.
Deeds, marry, deeds!
De Mau.   If you would deign to speak
Thus to your armies ere they march to battle,
Perchance your Eminence might have the pain
Of the throat-cutting to yourself.

Rich. [*aside*].   He has wit,
This Mauprat — [*Aloud.*] Let it pass; there is against you
What you can less excuse.] Messire de Mauprat,
Doom'd to sure death, how hast thou since consumed
The time allotted thee for serious thought
And solemn penitence?
   De Mau. [*embarrassed*]. The time, my lord?
   Rich. Is not the question plain? I'll answer for thee.
Thou hast sought nor priest nor shrine; no sackcloth
   chafed
Thy delicate flesh. The rosary and the death's-head
Have not, with pious meditation, purged
Earth from the carnal gaze. What thou hast *not* done
Brief told; what done, a volume! Wild debauch,
Turbulent riot; — for the morn the dice-box —
Noon claim'd the duel — and the night the wassail;
These, your most holy, pure preparatives,
For death and judgment. Do I wrong you, sir?
   De Mau. I was not always thus: — if changed my
      nature,
Blame that which changed my fate. — Alas, my lord,
There is a brotherhood which calm-eyed reason
Can wot not of betwixt despair and mirth.
My birth-place mid the vines of sunny Provence,
Perchance the stream that sparkles in my veins
Came from that wine of passionate life which, erst,
Glow'd in the wild heart of the troubadour:
And danger, which makes steadier courage wary,
But fevers me with an insane delight;
As one of old who on the mountain crags

Caught madness from a Mænad's haunting eyes.
Were you, my lord, — whose path imperial power,
And the grave cares of reverent wisdom, guard
From all that tempts to folly meaner men, —]
Were you accursed with that which you inflicted —
By bed and board, dogg'd by one ghastly spectre —
The while within you youth beat high, and life
Grew lovelier from the neighbouring frown of death —
The heart no bud, nor fruit — save in those seeds
Most worthless, which spring up, bloom, bear, and wither
In the same hour — Were this your fate, perchance,
You would have err'd like me!
  Rich.   I might, like you,
Have been a brawler and a reveller; — not,
Like you, a trickster and a thief. —
  De Mau. [*advancing threateningly*]. Lord Cardinal!
Unsay those words! —
     [HUGUET *deliberately raises the carbine.*
  Rich. [*waving his hand.*] Not quite so quick, friend
   Huguet;
Messire de Mauprat is a patient man,
And he can wait! —
      You have outrun your fortune; —
I blame you not, that you would be a beggar —
Each to his taste! — But I do charge you, sir,
That, being beggar'd, you would coin false moneys
Out of that crucible, called DEBT. — To live
On means not yours — be brave in silks and laces,
Gallant in steeds — splendid in banquets; — all
Not *yours* — ungiven — uninherited — unpaid for; —

This is to be a trickster; and to filch
Men's art and labour, which to them is wealth,
Life, daily bread, — quitting all scores with — "Friend,
You're troublesome!" — Why this, forgive me,
Is what — when done with a less dainty grace —
Plain folks call " *Theft!*" You owe eight thousand pistoles,
Minus one crown, two liards! —

    De Mau. [*aside*].   The old conjuror!
'Sdeath, he'll inform me next how many cups
I drank at dinner!

    Rich.   This is scandalous,
Shaming your birth and blood. I tell you, sir,
That you must pay your debts.

    De Mau.   With all my heart,
My lord. Where shall I borrow, then, the money?

    Rich. [*aside and laughing*]. A humorous dare-devil! —
    The very man
To suit my purpose — ready, frank, and bold!
                      [*Rising and earnestly.*
Adrien de Mauprat, men have called me cruel; —
I am not; — I am *just!* — I found France rent asunder, —
The rich men despots, and the poor banditti; —
Sloth in the mart, and schism within the temple;
Brawls festering to rebellion; and weak laws
Rotting away with rust in antique sheaths.
I have re-created France; and, from the ashes
Of the old feudal and decrepit carcase,
Civilization on her luminous wings
Soars, phœnix-like, to Jove! What was my art?
Genius, some say, — some, fortune, — witchcraft, some.

Not so; — my art was JUSTICE! — Force and fraud
Misname it cruelty — you shall confute them!
My champion you! You met me as your foe,
Depart my friend — You shall not die. — France needs
       you.
You shall wipe off all stains, — be rich, be honour'd,
Be great. —

    [DE MAUPRAT *falls on his knee —* RICHELIEU *raises him.*

    I ask, sir, in return, this hand,
To gift it with a bride, whose dower shall match,
Yet not exceed, her beauty.
    De Mau.   I, my lord, — [*hesitating*]
I have no wish to marry.
    Rich.   Surely, sir,
To die were worse.
    De Mau.   Scarcely; the poorest coward
Must die, — but knowingly to march to marriage —
My lord, it asks the courage of a lion!
    Rich. 'Traitor, thou triflest with me! I know *all!*
Thou hast dared to love my ward — my charge.
    De Mau.   As rivers
May love the sunlight — basking in the beams,
And hurrying on! —
    Rich.   Thou hast told her of thy love?
    De Mau. My lord, if I had dared to love a maid,
Lowliest in France, I would not so have wronged her,
As bid her link rich life and virgin hope
With one, the deathman's gripe might, from her side,
Pluck at the nuptial altar.

Rich.   I believe thee;
Yet since she knows not of thy love, renounce her;
Take life and fortune with another! — Silent?

De Mau. Your fate has been one triumph — you
            know not
How bless'd a thing it was in my dark hour
To nurse the one sweet thought you bid me banish.
Love hath no need of words; — nor less within
That holiest temple — the Heaven-builded soul —
Breathes the recorded vow. Base knight, — false lover
Were he, who barter'd all, that brighten'd grief,
Or sanctified despair, for life and gold.
Revoke your mercy; — I prefer the fate
I look'd for!

Rich.   Huguet! to the tapestry chamber
Conduct your prisoner. [*To* MAUPRAT.]
                  You will there behold
The executioner: — your doom be private —
And Heaven have mercy on you!

De Mau.   When I am dead,
Tell her, I loved her.

Rich.   Keep such follies, sir,
For fitter ears; — go —

De Mau.   Does he mock me?
              [*Exeunt* DE MAUPRAT, HUGUET.

Rich.   Joseph,
Come forth.
              Enter JOSEPH.
Methinks your cheek hath lost its rubies;

I fear you have been too lavish of the flesh;
The scourge is heavy.
 Joseph.   Pray you, change the subject.
 Rich. You good men are so modest! — Well, to
  business!
Go instantly — deeds — notaries! — bid my stewards
Arrange my house by the Luxembourg — *my* house
No more! — a bridal present to my ward,
Who weds to-morrow.
 Joseph.   Weds, with whom?
 Rich.   De Mauprat.
 Joseph. Penniless husband!
 Rich.   Bah! the mate for beauty
Should be a man, and not a money-chest!
When her brave sire lay on his bed of death,
I vow'd to be a father to his Julie: —
And so he died — the smile upon his lips! —
And when I spared the life of her young lover,
Methought I saw that smile again! — Who else,
Look you, in all the court — who else so well,
Brave, or supplant the favourite; — balk the king —
Baffle their schemes? — I have tried him: — He has
  honour
And courage; — qualities that eagle-plume
Men's souls, — and fit them for the fiercest sun,
Which ever melted the weak waxen minds
That flutter in the beams of gaudy Power!
Besides, he has taste, this Mauprat: — When my play
Was acted to dull tiers of lifeless gapers,*

 * The Abbé Arnand tells us that the queen was a little avenged on

Who had no soul for poetry, I saw him
Applaud in the proper places: — trust me, Joseph,
He is a man of an uncommon promise!
 Joseph. And yet your foe.
 Rich.   Have I not foes enow? —
Great men gain doubly when they make foes friends.
Remember my grand maxims: — First employ
All methods to conciliate.*
 Joseph.   Failing these?
 Rich. [*fiercely*]. All means to crush: as with the
  opening, and
The clenching of this little hand, I will
Crush the small venom of these stinging courtiers.
So, so, we've baffled Baradas.
 Joseph.   And when
Check the conspiracy?

---

the cardinal by the ill success of the tragi-comedy of "Mirame" — more than suspected to be his own — though presented to the world under the foster-name of Desmarets. Its representation (says Pelisson) cost him 300,000 crowns. He was so transported out of himself by the performance, that at one time he thrust his person half out of his box to show himself to the assembly; at another time he imposed silence on the audience, that they might not lose "*des endroits encore plus beaux!*" He said afterwards to Desmarets: — "Eh bien, les Français n'auront donc jamais de goût. Ils n'ont pas été charmés de Mirame!" Arnaud says pithily, — "On ne pouvoit alors avoir d'autre satisfaction des offenses d'un homme qui étoit maître de tout, et redoutable à tout le monde." Nevertheless, his style in prose, though not devoid of the pedantic affectations of the time, often rises into very noble eloquence.

 * "Vinisrt remarque une chose qui peut expliquer la conduite de Richelieu en d'autres circonstances: — c'est que les seigneurs à qui leur naissance ou leur mérite pouvoit permettre des prétensions, il avoit pour système, de leur accorder au-delà même de leurs droits et de leurs espérances, mais, aussi, une fois comblés — si, au lieu de reconnoître ses services ils se levoient contre lui, et ils traitoit sans miséricorde." — *Anquetil. See* also the Political Testament, and the Mémoires de Cardinal Richelieu, in Petitot's collection.

Rich. Check, check? Full way to it.
Let it bud, ripen, flaunt i' the day, and burst
To fruit, — the Dead Sea's fruit of ashes; ashes
Which I will scatter to the winds.
                    Go, Joseph;
When you return, I have a feast for you;
The last great act of my great play: the verses,
Methinks, are fine, — ah, very fine. — You write
Verses!* — [*aside*] such verses! — You have wit,
    discernment.
Joseph [*aside*]. Worse than the scourge! Strange
    that so great a statesman
Should be so bad a poet.
    Rich.   What dost thou say?
Joseph. That it is strange so great a statesman
    should
Be so sublime a poet.
    Rich.   Ah, you rogue;
Laws die, Books never. Of my ministry
I am not vain! but of my muse, I own it.
Come, you shall hear the verses now. [*Takes up a MS.*
    Joseph.   My lord,
The deeds, the notaries!

---

* "Tantôt fanatique — tantôt fourbe — fondeur les religieuses de Calvaire — faire des vers." Thus speaks Voltaire of Father Joseph. His talents and influence with Richelieu, grossly exaggerated in his own day, are now rightly estimated.
"C'étoit en effet un homme infatigable — portant dans les entreprises, l'activité, la souplesse, l'opiniâtreté propre à les faire réussir." — *Anquetil*.
He wrote a Latin poem, called "La Turciade," in which he sought to excite the kingdoms of Christendom against the Turks. But the inspiration of Tyrtæus was denied to Father Joseph.

Rich.   True, I pity you;
But business first, then pleasure.   [*Exit* Joseph.
Rich. [*seats himself and reading*]. Ah, sublime!

          Enter De Mauprat *and* Julie.

De Mau. Oh, speak, my lord — I dare not think
     you mock me.
And yet —
   Rich. Hush — hush — This line must be consider'd!
Julie. Are we not both your children?
   Rich.   What a couplet! —
How now! Oh, sir — you live!
   De Mau.   Why, no, methinks,
Elysium is not life!
   Julie.   He smiles! — you smile,
My father! From my heart for ever, now,
I'll blot the name of orphan!
   Rich.   Rise, my children,
For ye are mine — mine both; — and in your sweet
And young delight — your love (life's first-born glory) —
My own lost youth breathes musical!
   De Mau.   I'll seek
Temple and priest henceforward, were it but
To learn Heaven's choicest blessings.
   Rich.   Thou shalt seek
Temple and priest right soon; the morrow's sun
Shall see across these barren thresholds pass
The fairest bride in Paris. — Go, my children,
Even *I* loved once! — Be lovers while ye may!

How is it with you, sir! You bear it bravely:
You know, it asks the courage of a lion.
                    [*Exeunt* JULIE *and* DE MAUPRAT.
    Rich. Oh godlike Power! Woe, Rapture, Penury,
        Wealth, —
Marriage and Death, for one infirm old man
Through a great empire to dispense — withhold —
As the will whispers! And shall things — like motes
That live in my daylight — lackeys of court wages,
Dwarf'd starvelings — manikins, upon whose shoulders
The burthen of a province were a load
More heavy than the globe on Atlas, — cast
Lots for my robes and sceptre? France! I love thee!
All Earth shall never pluck thee from my heart!'
My mistress France — my wedded wife, — sweet
    France,
Who shall proclaim divorce for thee and me!
                        [*Exit* RICHELIEU.

ACT II.

SECOND DAY.

SCENE I. — *A splendid apartment in* MAUPRAT'S *new House. Casements opening to the Gardens, beyond which the domes of the Luxembourg Palace.*

Enter BARADAS.
    Bar. Mauprat's new home: — too splendid for a
        soldier!
But o'er his floors — the while I stalk — methinks
My shadow spreads gigantic to the gloom

The old rude towers of the Bastile cast far
Along the smoothness of the jocund day. —
Well, thou hast 'scaped the fierce caprice of Richelieu;
But art thou farther from the headsman, fool?
Thy secret I have whisper'd to the king;
Thy marriage makes the king thy foe. — Thou stand'st
On the abyss — and in the pool below
I see a ghastly, headless phantom mirror'd; —
Thy likeness ere the marriage moon hath waned.
Meanwhile — meanwhile — ha — ha, if thou art wedded,
Thou art not wived.

   Enter MAUPRAT [*splendidly dressed*].

 De Mau.   Was ever fate like mine?
So blest and yet so wretched!
 Bar.   Joy, De Mauprat! —
Why, what a brow, man, for your wedding-day!
 De Mau. Jest not! — Distraction!
 Bar.   What, your wife a shrew
Already? Courage, man — the common lot!
 De Mau. Oh! that she were less lovely, or less loved!
 Bar. Riddles again!
 De Mau.   You know what chanced between
The cardinal and myself.
 Bar.   This morning brought
Your letter: — faith, a strange account! I laugh'd
And wept at once for gladness.
 De Mau. . We were wed
At noon; — the rite perform'd, came hither! — scarce
Arrived, when —

Bar. Well? —

De Mau. Wide flew the doors, and lo, Messire de Beringhen, and this epistle!

Bar. 'Tis the king's hand! — the royal seal!

De Mau. Read — read —

Bar. [*reading.*] "Whereas Adrien de Mauprat, Colonel and Chevalier in our armies, being already guilty of High Treason, by the seizure of our town of Faviaux, has presumed, without our knowledge, consent, or sanction, to connect himself by marriage with Julie de Mortemar, a wealthy orphan, attached to the person of Her Majesty, without our knowledge or consent — We do hereby proclaim and declare the said marriage contrary to law. On penalty of death, Adrien de Mauprat will not communicate with the said Julie de Mortemar by word or letter, save in the presence of our faithful servant, the Sieur de Beringhen, and then with such respect and decorum as are due to a demoiselle attached to the Court of France, until such time as it may suit our royal pleasure to confer with the Holy Church on the formal annulment of the marriage, and with our Council on the punishment to be awarded to Messire de Mauprat, who is cautioned, for his own sake, to preserve silence as to our injunction, more especially to Mademoiselle de Mortemar.

"Given under our hand and seal at the Louvre.

"Louis."

Bar. [*returning the letter*]. Amazement! — Did not
    Richelieu say, the king
Knew not your crime?

De Mau.   He said so.

Bar.   Poor De Mauprat! —
See you the snare, the vengeance worse than death,
Of which you are the victim?

De Mau.   Ha!

Bar. [*aside.*]   It works!
        [JULIE *and* DE BERINGHEN *in the Gardens.*
You have not sought the cardinal yet to —

De Mau.   No!
Scarce yet my sense awaken'd from the shock;
Now I will seek him.

Bar.   Hold, beware! — Stir not
Till we confer again.

De Mau.   Speak — out, man!

Bar.   Hush!
Your wife! — De Beringhen! — Be on your guard —
Obey the royal orders to the letter.
I'll look around your palace. By my troth
A princely mansion!

De Mau.   Stay —

Bar.   So new a bridegroom
Can want no visitors; — Your servant, madam!
Oh! happy pair — Oh! charming picture!
                    [*Exit through a side-door.*

Julie.   Adrien,
You left us suddenly — Are you not well?

De Mau. Oh, very well — that is — extremely ill!

Julie. Ill, Adrien?   [*Taking his hand.*

De Mau.   Not when I see thee.

[*He is about to lift her hand to his lips when* DE BERINGHEN *coughs and pulls his mantle.* MAUPRAT *drops the hand and walks away.*

Julie.   Alas!
Should he not love me?
   De Ber. [*aside.*] Have a care; I must
Report each word — each gesture to his Majesty.
   De Mau. Sir, if you were not in his Majesty's service,
You'd be the most officious, impudent,
Damn'd busy-body ever interfering
In a man's family affairs.
   De Ber.   But as
I do belong, sir, to his Majesty —
   De Mau. You're lucky! — Still, were we a story
       higher,
'Twere prudent not to go too near the window.
   Julie. Adrien, what have I done? Say, am I
       changed
Since yesterday? — or was it but for wealth,
Ambition, life — that — that — you swore you loved me?
   De Mau. I shall go mad! — I do, indeed I do —
   De Ber. [*aside.*] Not love her! that were highly disrespectful.
   Julie. You do — what, Adrien?
   De Mau.   Oh! I do, indeed —
I do think, that this weather is delightful!
A charming day! the sky is so serene!
And what a prospect! — [*to* DE BERINGHEN] Oh! you
       popinjay!

Julie. He jests at me! — he mocks me! — yet I
    love him,
And every look becomes the lips we love!
Perhaps I am too grave? — You laugh at Julie;
If laughter please you, welcome be the music!
Only say, Adrien, that you love me.
    De Mau. [*kissing her hand.*]   Ay;
With my whole heart I love you! —
                                Now, sir, go,
And tell that to his Majesty! — Who ever
Heard of its being a state offence to kiss
·The hand of one's own wife?
    Julie.   He says he loves me,
And starts away, as if to say "I love you"
Meant something *very* dreadful. — Come, sit by me, —
I place your chair! — fie on your gallantry!

    [*They sit down; as he pushes his chair back, she draws
    hers nearer.*

Why must this strange Messire de Beringhen
Be always here? He never takes a hint.
Do you not wish him gone?
    De Mau.   Upon my soul
I do, my Julie! — Send him for your *bouquet*,
Your glove, your — anything.
    Julie.   Messire de Beringhen,
I dropp'd my glove in the gardens by the fountain,
Or the alcove, or — stay — no, by the statue
Of Cupid; may I ask you to —
    De Ber.   To send for it?

Certainly [*ringing a bell on the table.*] André, Pierre,
    (your rascals, how
Do ye call them?)

Enter Servants.

          Ah — *Madame* has dropp'd her glove
In the gardens, by the fountain, — or the alcove;
Or — stay — no, by the statue — eh? — of Cupid.
Bring it.
  De Mau. Did ever now one pair of shoulders
Carry such waggon-loads of impudence
Into a gentleman's drawing-room?
                       Dear Julie,
I'm busy — letters — visitors — the devil!
I do beseech you leave me — I say — leave me.
  Julie [*weeping.*] You are unkind.   [*Exit.*
    [*As she goes out,* Mauprat *drops on one knee and kisses
    the hem of her mantle, unseen by her.*

  De Ber.   Ten millions of apologies —
  De Mau. I'll not take one of them. I have, as yet,
Withstood all things — my heart — my love — my rights.
But Julie's tears! — When is this farce to end?
  De Ber. Oh! when you please. His Majesty re-
    quests me,
As soon as you infringe his gracious orders,
To introduce you to the Governor
Of the Bastile. I should have had that honour
Before, but, gad, my foible is good-nature;
One can't be hard upon a friend's infirmities.

De Mau. I know the king can send me to the scaf-
    fold —
Dark prospect! — but I'm used to it; and if
The Church and Council, by this hour to-morrow,
One way or other settle not the matter,
I will —
    De Ber. What, my dear sir?
    De Mau.   Show you the door,
My dear, dear sir; talk as I please, with whom
I please, in my own house, dear sir, until
His Majesty shall condescend to find
A stouter gentleman than you, dear sir,
To take me out; and now you understand me,
My dear, most dear — oh damnably dear sir!
    De Ber. What, almost in a passion! you will cool
Upon reflection. Well, since *Madame's* absent,
I'll take a small refreshment. Now, don't stir;
Be careful; — how's your burgundy? — I'll taste it —
Finish it all before I leave you. Nay,
No form; — you see I make myself at home.
                    [*Exit* DE BERINGHEN.
    De Mau. [*going to the door through which* BARADAS
    had passed.] Baradas! Count!

            Enter BARADAS.

            You spoke of snares — of vengeance
Sharper than death — be plainer.
    Bar.   What so clear?
Richelieu has but two passions —
    De Mau.   Richelieu!

Bar.   Yes!
Ambition and revenge — in you both blended.
First for ambition — Julie is his ward,
Innocent — docile — pliant to his will —
He placed her at the court — foresaw the rest —
The king loves Julie!
    De Mau.   Merciful Heaven! The king!
    Bar. Such Cupids lend new plumes to Richelieu's wings:
But the court etiquette must give such Cupids
The veil of Hymen — (Hymen but in name.)
He look'd abroad — found you his foe: — *thus* served
Ambition — by the grandeur of his ward,
And vengeance — by dishonour to his foe!
    De Mau. Prove this.
    Bar.   You have the proof — the royal Letter: —
Your strange exemption from the general pardon,
Known but to me and Richelieu; can you doubt
Your friend to acquit your foe? The truth is glaring —
Richelieu alone could tell the princely lover
The tale which sells your life, — or buys your honour!
    De Mau. I see it all! Mock pardon — hurried nuptials —
False bounty! — all! — the serpent of that smile!
Oh! it stings home!
    Bar.   You yet shall crush his malice;
Our plans are sure: — Orleans is at our head;
We meet to-night; join us, and with us triumph.

De Mau. *To-night?* — Oh, Heaven! — my mar-
 riage night! — Revenge!
Bar. [What class of men, whose white lips do not
 curse
The grim, insatiate, universal tyrant?
We, noble-born — where are our antique rights —
Our feudal seigniories — our castled strength,
That did divide us from the base Plebeians,
And made our swords our law — where are they? Trod
To dust — and o'er the graves of our dead power
Scaffolds are monuments — the kingly house
Shorn of its beams — the Royal Sun of France
'Clipsed by this blood-red comet. Where we turn,
Nothing but Richelieu! — armies — church — state —
 laws,
But mirrors that do multiply his beams.
He sees all — acts all — Argus and Briareus —
Spy at our boards — and deathsman at our hearths;
Under the venom of one laidley nightshade,
Wither the lilies of all France.
 De Mau. [*impatiently*].   But Julie —
 Bar. [*unheeding him*]. As yet the Fiend that serves
 hath saved his power
From every snare; and in the epitaphs
Of many victims dwells a warning moral
That preaches caution. Were I not assured
That what before was hope is ripen'd now
Into most certain safety, trust me, Mauprat,
I still could hush my hate and mark thy wrongs,
And say "Be patient!" *Now,* the King himself

Smiles kindly when I tell him that his peers
Will rid him of his Priest. You knit your brows,
Noble impatience! — Pass we to our scheme!]
'Tis Richelieu's wont, each morn, within his chapel
(Hypocrite worship ended), to dispense
Alms to the Mendicant-friars, — in that guise
A band (yourself the leader) shall surround
And seize the despot.
  De Mau.   But the king? — but Julie?
  Bar. The king, infirm in health, in mind more
    feeble,
Is but the plaything of a minister's will.
Were Richelieu dead — his power were mine; and
  Louis
Soon should forget his passion and your crime.
But whither now?
  De Mau.   I know not; I scarce hear thee;
A little while for thought: anon I'll join thee;
But now, all air seems tainted, and I loathe
The face of man!
     [*Exit* DE MAUPRAT *through the Gardens.*
  Bar.   Start from the chase, my prey,
But as thou speed'st the hell-hounds of revenge
Pant in thy track and dog thee down.

  Enter DE BERINGHEN, *his mouth full, a napkin in*
    his hand.
  De Ber. •   Chevalier,
Your cook's a miracle, — what, my host gone?
Faith, count, my office is a post of danger —

A fiery fellow, Mauprat! touch and go, —
Match and saltpetre, — pr—r — r—r — !
  Bar.   You
Will be released ere long. The king resolves
To call the bride to court this day.
  De Ber.   Poor Mauprat!
Yet, since *you* love the lady, why so careless
Of the king's suit?
  Bar.   Because the lady's virtuous,
And the king timid. Ere he win the suit,
He'll lose the crown, — the bride will be a widow, —
And I — the Richelieu of the Regent Orleans.
  De Ber. Is Louis still so chafed against the Fox
For snatching yon fair dainty from the Lion?
  Bar. So chafed, that Richelieu totters. Yes, the
    king
Is half conspirator against the cardinal.
Enough of this. I've found the man we wanted, —
The man to head the hands that murder Richelieu, —
The man, whose name the synonym for daring.
  De Ber. He must mean me! No, count; I am, I own,
A valiant dog — but still —
  Bar.   Whom can I mean.
But Mauprat? — Mark, to-night we meet at Marion's.
There shall we sign; thence send this scroll [*showing it*]
    to Bouillon.
You're in that secret [*affectionately*] — one of our new
    Council.
  De Ber. But to admit the Spaniard — France's
    foe —

Into the heart of France — dethrone the king —
It looks like treason, and I smell the headsman.

Bar. Oh, sir, too late to falter: when we meet
We must arrange the separate, coarser scheme,
For Richelieu's death. Of this despatch De Mauprat
Must nothing learn. He only bites at vengeance,
And he would start from treason. — We must post him
Without the door at Marion's — as a sentry.
[*Aside*] — So, when his head is on the block — his
    tongue
Cannot betray our more august designs!

De Ber. I'll meet you if the king can spare me. —
    [*Aside.*] No!
I am too old a goose to play with foxes,
I'll roost at home. Meanwhile, in the next room
There's a delicious pâté, — let's discuss it.

Bar. Pshaw! a man fill'd with a sublime ambition
Has no time to discuss your pâtés.

De Ber.   Pshaw!
And a man fill'd with as sublime a pâté
Has no time to discuss ambition. — Gad,
I have the best of it!

    Enter JULIE *hastily with first* Courtier.

Julie [*to* Courtier]. A summons, sir,
To attend the Louvre? — On *this* day, too?

Cour.   Madame,
The royal carriage waits below. — Messire [*to* DE BERIN-
    GHEN]
You will return with us.

Julie. What can this mean? —
Where is my husband?

Bar. He has left the house,
Perhaps till nightfall — so he bade me tell you.
Alas, were I the lord of such fair treasure —

Julie [*impatiently*]. Till nightfall? — Strange — my
heart misgives me!

Cour. Madam,
My orders will not broke delay.

Julie [*to* BARADAS]. You'll see him —
And you will tell him!

Bar. From the flowers of Hybla
Never more gladly did the bee bear honey,
Than I take sweetness from those rosiest lips,
Though to the hive of others!

Cour. [*to* DE BERINGHEN]. Come, Messire.

De Ber. [*hesitating*]. One moment, just to —

Cour. Come, sir.

De Ber. I shall not
Discuss the pâté after all. 'Ecod,
I'm puzzled now. I don't know who's the best of it!
[*Exeunt* JULIE, DE BERINGHEN, *and* Courtier.

Bar. Now will this fire his fever into madness!
All is made clear: Mauprat *must* murder Richelieu —
Die for that crime: — I shall console his Julie —
This will reach Bouillon! — from the wrecks of France
I shall carve out — who knows — perchance a throne!
All in despite of my Lord Cardinal. —

Enter DE MAUPRAT *from the Gardens.*

De Mau. Speak! can it be? — Methought, that from the terrace
I saw the carriage of the king — and Julie!
No! — no! my frenzy peoples the void air
With its own phantoms!
Bar. Nay, too true. — Alas!
Was ever lightning swifter, or more blasting,
Than Richelieu's forkèd guile?
De Mau. I'll to the Louvre —
Bar. And lose all hope! — The Louvre! — the sure gate
To the Bastile!
De Mau. The king —
Bar. Is but the wax,
Which Richelieu stamps! Break the malignant *seal*,
And I will rase the print. Come, man, take heart!
Her virtue well could brave a sterner trial
Than a few hours of cold imperious courtship.
Were Richelieu *dust* — no danger!
De Mau. Ghastly Vengeance!
To thee, and thine august and solemn sister,
The unrelenting Death, I dedicate
The blood of Armand Richelieu! When Dishonour
Reaches our hearths Law dies and Murther takes
The angel shape of Justice!
Bar. Bravely said!
At midnight, — Marion's! — Nay, I cannot leave thee
To thoughts that —

De Mau.   Speak not to me! — I am yours! —
But speak not! There's a voice within my soul,
Whose cry could drown the thunder. — Oh! if men
Will play dark sorcery with the heart of man
Let them, who raise the spell, beware the Fiend! [*Exeunt.*

SCENE II.

A room in the Palais Cardinal (as in the First Act.)

RICHELIEU *and* JOSEPH.

FRANÇOIS *writing at a table.*

Joseph. Yes; — Huguet, taking his accustom'd
          round, —
Disguised as some plain burgher, — heard these rufflers
Quoting your name: — he listen'd, — "Pshaw," said one,
"We are to seize the Cardinal in his palace
To-morrow!" — "How?" the other ask'd: — "You'll
          hear
The whole design to-night: the Duke of Orleans
And Baradas have got the map of action
At their fingers' end." — "So be it," quoth the other,
"I will be there, — Marion de Lorme's — at mid-
          night!"

Rich. I have them, man, — I have them!

Joseph   So they say
Of you, my lord; — believe me, that their plans
Are mightier than you deem. You must employ
Means no less vast to meet them!

Rich.   Bah! in policy
We foil gigantic danger, not by giants,

4*

52   RICHELIEU;   [ACT II.

But dwarfs. — The statues of our stately fortune
Are sculptured by the chisel — not the axe!*
Ah! were I younger — by the knightly heart
That beats beneath these priestly robes,** I would
Have pastime with these cut-throats! — Yea, — as when
Lured to the ambush of the expecting foe, —
I clove my pathway through the plumed sea!
Reach me yon falchion, François, — not that bauble
For carpet-warriors, — yonder — such a blade
As old Charles Martel might have wielded when
He drove the Saracen from France.

    [FRANÇOIS *brings him one of the long two-handed swords
      worn in the middle ages.*

                                    With this
I, at Rochelle, did hand to hand engage

---

* Richelieu not only employed the lowest, but would often consult men commonly esteemed the dullest. "Il disait que dans des choses de très grande importance, il avait expérimenté, que les moins sages donnaient souvent les meilleurs expédiens." — *Le Clerc.*

** Both Richelieu and Joseph were originally intended for the profession of arms. Joseph had served before he obeyed the spiritual inspiration to become a Capuchin. The death of his brother opened to Richelieu the bishopric of Luçon; but his military propensities were as strong as his priestly ambition. I need scarcely add that the cardinal, during his brilliant campaign in Italy, marched at the head of his troops in complete armour. It was under his administration that occurs the last example of proclaiming war by the chivalric defiance of herald and cartel. Richelieu valued himself much on his personal activity, — for his vanity was as universal as his ambition. A nobleman of the house of Grammont one day found him employed in *jumping*, and with all the *savoir vivre* of a Frenchman and a courtier, offered to jump against him. He suffered the cardinal to jump higher, and soon after found himself rewarded by an appointment. Yet, strangely enough, this vanity did not lead to a patronage injurious to the state; for never before in France was ability made so essential a requisite in promotion. He was lucky in finding the cleverest fellow among his adroitest flatterers

The stalwart Englisher, — no mongrels, boy,
Those island mastiffs, — mark the notch — a deep
    one —
His casque made here, — I shore him to the waist!
A toy — a feather — then! [*Tries to wield, and lets it fall.*
                      You see, a child could
Slay Richelieu now.
    Fran. [*his hand on his hilt*]. But *now*, at your command
Are other weapons, my good lord.
    Rich. [*who has seated himself as to write, lifts the pen.*]
                      True, — THIS!
Beneath the rule of men entirely great
The pen is mightier than the sword. Behold
The arch-enchanter's wand! — itself a nothing! —
But taking sorcery from the master-hand
To paralyse the Cæsars — and to strike
The loud earth breathless! — Take away the sword —
States can be saved without it! [*Looking on the clock.*
                 'Tis the hour, —
Retire, sir.   [*Exit* FRANÇOIS.
    [*A knock is heard. A door concealed in the arras opens
    cautiously. Enter* MARION DE LORME.

    Joseph [*amazed*]. Marion de Lorme!
    Rich.   Hist! Joseph!
Keep guard.
              [JOSEPH *retires to the principal entrance.*
    My faithful Marion!
    Marion.   Good, my Lord,
They meet to-night in my poor house. The Duke
Of Orleans heads them.

Rich. Yes, go on.
Marion. His Highness
Much question'd if I knew some brave, discreet,
And vigilant man, whose tongue could keep a secret,
And who had those twin qualities for service,
The love of gold, the hate of Richelieu. —
Rich. You? —
Marion. Made answer, "Yes — my brother; — bold
and trusty;
Whose faith, my faith could pledge;" — the Duke then
bade me
Have him equipp'd and arm'd — well mounted — ready
This night to part for Italy.
Rich. Aha! —
Has Bouillon too turn'd traitor? — So, methought! —
What part of Italy?
Marion. The Piedmont frontier,
Where Bouillon lies encamp'd.
Rich. Now there is danger!
Great danger! — If he tamper with the Spaniard,
And Louis list not to my counsel, as,
Without sure proof, he will not, — France is lost.
What more?
Marion. Dark hints of some design to seize
Your person in your palace. Nothing clear —
His Highness trembled while he spoke — the words
Did choke each other.
Rich. So! — Who is the brother
You recommended to the Duke?

Marion.   Whoever
Your Eminence may father! —
Rich.   Darling Marion!*
[*Goes to the table, and returns with a large bag of gold.*
There — pshaw — a trifle! — What an eye you have!
And what a smile — child! [*kisses her.*] — Ah! you
     fair perdition —
'Tis well I'm old!
    Marion [*aside and seriously*]. What a great man he is!
    Rich. You are sure they meet? — the hour?
    Marion.   At midnight.
    Rich.   And
You will engage to give the Duke's Despatch
To whom I send?
    Marion.   Ay, marry!
    Rich. [*aside*].   Huguet? No;
He will be wanted elsewhere. — Joseph? — zealous,
But too well known — too much the *elder* brother!
Mauprat? — alas! it is his wedding-day! —
François? — the Man of Men! — unnoted — young —
Ambitious — [*Goes to the door.*] — François!

* Voltaire openly charges Richelieu with being the lover of Marion de Lorme; and the great poet of France, Victor Hugo, has sacrificed History to adorn her with qualities which were certainly not added to her personal charms. She was not less perfidious than beautiful. Le Clerc, properly, refutes the accusation of Voltaire against the discretion of Richelieu, and says, very justly, that if the great minister had the frailties of human nature, he learnt how to veil them, — at least when he obtained the scarlet. In earlier life he had been prone to gallantries which a little prepossessed the king (who was formal and decorous, and threw a singular coldness into the few attachments he permitted to himself), against the aspiring intriguer. But these gayer occupations died away in the engagement of higher pursuits or of darker passions.

Enter FRANÇOIS.

Rich. Follow this fair lady;
(Find him the suiting garments, Marion,) take
My fleetest steed: — arm thyself to the teeth;
A packet will be given you — with orders,
No matter what! — The instant that your hand
Closes upon it — clutch *it*, like your honour,
Which Death alone can steal, or ravish — set
Spurs to your steed — be breathless, till you stand
Again before me. — Stay, sir! — You will find me
Two short leagues hence — at Ruelle, in my castle.
Young man, be blithe! — for — note me — from the
    hour
I grasp that packet — think your guardian Star
Rains fortune on you! —
    Fran. If I fail —
    Rich. Fail — fail!
In the lexicon of youth, which Fate reserves
For a bright manhood, there is no such word
As — *fail!* — (You will instruct him further, Marion)
Follow her — but at distance; — speak not to her,
Till you are housed. — Farewell, boy! Never say
"*Fail*" again.
    Fran. I will not!
    Rich. [*patting his locks*]. There's my young hero! —
                      [*Exeunt* FRANÇOIS, MARION.
    Rich. So, they would seize my person in this palace? —
I cannot guess their scheme; but my retinue
Is here too large! — a single traitor could

Strike impotent the faith of thousands; — Joseph,
Art sure of Huguet? — Think — we hang'd his Father!
  Joseph. But you have bought the Son; — heap'd
    favours on him!
  Rich. Trash! — favours past — that's nothing. —
    In his hours
Of confidence with you, has he named the favours
To *come* — he counts on?
  Joseph.   Yes: — a Colonel's rank,
And Letters of Nobility.
  Rich.   What, Huguet! —
    [*Here* Huguet *enters, as to address the* Cardinal, *who
    does not perceive him.*]
  Hug. My own name, soft — [*glides behind the screen*].
  Rich.   Colonel and Nobleman!
My bashful Huguet — that can never be! —
We have him not the less — we'll *promise it!*
And see the King withholds! — Ah, kings are oft
A great convenience to a minister!
No wrong to Huguet either; — Moralists
Say, Hope is sweeter than Possession! — Yes! —
We'll count on Huguet! Favours *past* do gorge
Our dogs! leave service drowsy — dull the scent,
Slacken the speed; — favours *to come*, my Joseph,
Produce a lusty, hungry gratitude,
A ravenous zeal, that of the commonest cur
Would make a Cerberus. — You are right, this treason
Assumes a fearful aspect: — but once crush'd,
Its very ashes shall manure the soil
Of power; and ripen such full sheaves of greatness,

That all the summer of my fate shall seem
Fruitless beside the autumn!
  [HUGUET *holds up his hand menacingly, and creeps out.*
 Joseph.   The saints grant it!
 Rich. [*solemnly*]. Yes — for sweet France, Heaven
   grant it! — O my country,
For thee — thee only — though men deem it not —
Are toil and terror my familiars! — I
Have made thee great and fair — upon thy brows
Wreath'd the old Roman laurel: — at thy feet
Bow'd nations down. — No pulse in my ambition
Whose beatings were not measured from thy heart!
[In the old times before us, patriots lived
And died for liberty —
 Joseph.   As you would live
And die for despotry —
 Rich.   False monk, not so,
But for the purple and the power wherein
State clothes herself. — I love my native land
Not as Venetian, Englisher, or Swiss,
But as a Noble and a Priest of France;
"All things for France" — lo, my eternal maxim!
The vital axle of the restless wheels
That bear me on! With her I have entwined
My passions and my fate — my crimes — my virtues —
Hated and loved,[*] and schemed, and shed men's blood,

---

[*] Richelieu did in fact so thoroughly associate himself with the State, that in cases where the extreme penalty of the law had been incurred, Le Clerc justly observes that he was more inexorable to those he had favoured — even to his own connections — than to other and more indifferent offenders. It must be remembered, as some excuse for his un-

As the calm crafts of Tuscan Sages teach
Those who would make their country great. Beyond
The map of France — my heart can travel not,
But fills that limit to its farthest verge;
And while I live — Richelieu and France are one.}

relenting sternness, that before his time the great had been accustomed to commit any disorder with impunity, even the crime of treason;" — "auparavant on ne faisoit poser les armes aux rebelles qu'en leur accordant quelque récompense." On entering into the administration, he therefore laid it down as a maxim necessary to the existence of the State, that "no crime should be committed with impunity." To carry out this maxim, the long-established license to crime made even justice seem cruel. But the victims most commiserated, from their birth or accomplishments, as Montmorenci, or Cinq Mars, were traitors in actual conspiracy against their country, and would have forfeited life in any land where the punishment of death existed, and the lawgiver was strong enough to vindicate the law. Richelieu was, in fact, a patriot unsoftened by philanthropy. As in Venice (where the favourite aphorism was — "Venice first, Christianity next,"*) so, with Richelieu, the primary consideration was, "What will be best for the country?" He had no abstract principle, whether as a politician or a priest, when applied to the world that lay beyond the boundaries of France. Thus he, whose object was to found in France a splendid and imperious despotism, assisted the Parliamentary party in England, and signed a treaty of alliance and subsidies with the Catalan rebels, for the establishment of a republic in Barcelona: to convulse other monarchies was to consolidate the growing monarchy of France. So he, who completely crushed the Protestant party at home, braved all the wrath of the Vatican, and even the resentment of the King, in giving the most essential aid to the Protestants abroad. There was, indeed, a largeness of view in his hostility to the French Huguenots, which must be carefully distinguished from the intolerance of the mere priest. He opposed them, not as a Catholic, but as a statesman. The Huguenots were strong republicans, and had formed plans for dividing France into provincial commonwealths; and the existence of Rochelle was absolutely incompatible with the integrity of the French monarchy. It was a second capital, held by the Huguenots, claiming independent authority and the right to treat with foreign powers. Richelieu's final conquest was marked by a humanity that had nothing of the bigot. The Huguenots obtained a complete amnesty, and had only to regret the loss of privileges and fortifications which could not have existed with any security to the rest of France.

* "Prin Veneziani, poi Christiano."

We Priests, to whom the Church forbids in youth
The plighted one — to manhood's toil denies
The soother helpmate — from our wither'd age
Shuts the sweet blossoms of the second spring
That smiles in the name of Father — we are yet
Not holier than Humanity, and must
Fulfil Humanity's condition — Love!
Debarred the Actual, we but breathe a life
To the chill Marble of the Ideal — Thus,
In thy unseen and abstract Majesty,
My France, my Country, I have bodied forth
A thing to love. What are these robes of state,
This pomp, this palace? perishable baubles!
In this world two things only are immortal —
Fame and a People!

Enter HUGUET.

Hug. My Lord Cardinal,
Your Eminence bade me seek you at this hour.

Rich. Did I? — True, Huguet. — So — you overheard
Strange talk amongst these gallants? Snares and traps
For Richelieu? — Well — we'll balk them; let me think —
The men-at-arms you head — how many?

Hug. Twenty,*
My Lord.

---

* The guard attached to Richelieu's person was, in the first instance, fifty arquebusiers, afterwards increased to two companies of cavalry and two hundred musqueteers. Huguet is therefore to be considered merely as the lieutenant of a small detachment of this little army. In point of fact, the subdivisions of the guard took it in turns to serve.

Rich. All trusty?
Hug. Yes, for ordinary
Occasions — if for great ones, I would change
Three-fourths at least.
Rich. Ay, what are great occasions?
Hug. Great bribes!
Rich. [*to* JOSEPH]. Good lack, he knows some paragons
Superior to great bribes!
Hug. True Gentlemen
Who have transgress'd the laws — and value life
And lack not gold; your Eminence alone
Can grant them pardon. *Ergo*, you can trust them!
Rich. Logic! — So be it — let this *honest* twenty
Be arm'd and mounted. — [*Aside.*] So they meet at midnight.
The attempt on me to-morrow — Ho! we'll strike
'Twixt wind and water. — [*Aloud.*] Does it need much time
To find these ornaments to Human Nature?
Hug. My Lord — the trustiest of them are not birds
That love the daylight. — I do know a haunt
Where they meet nightly —
Rich. Ere the dawn be grey,
All could be arm'd, assembled, and at Ruelle
In my old hall?
Hug. By one hour after midnight.
Rich. The castle's strong. You know its outlets, Huguet?
Would twenty men, well posted, keep such guard

That not one step — (and Murther's step is stealthy)—
Could glide within — unseen?
 Hug.   A triple wall —
A drawbridge and portcullis — twenty men
Under my lead, a month might hold that castle
Against a host.
 Rich. They do not strike till morning,
Yet I will shift the quarter — Bid the grooms
Prepare the litter — I will hence to Ruelle
While daylight last — and one hour after midnight
You and your twenty saints shall seek me thither!
You're made to rise! — You are, sir; — eyes of lynx,
Ears of the stag, a footfall like the snow;
You are a valiant fellow; — yea, a trusty,
Religious, exemplary, incorrupt,
And precious jewel of a fellow, Huguet!
If I live long enough, — ay, mark my words —
If I live long enough, you'll be a Colonel —
Noble, perhaps! — One hour, sir, after midnight.
 Hug. You leave me dumb with gratitude, my Lord;
I'll pick the trustiest — [*aside.*] Marion's house can furnish!
          [*Exit* HUGUET.
 Rich. How like a spider shall I sit in my hole,
And watch the meshes tremble.
 Joseph.   But, my Lord,
Were it not wiser still to man the palace,
And seize the traitors in the act?
 Rich.   No; Louis,
Long chafed against me — Julie stolen from him,
Will rouse him more. He'll say I hatch'd the treason,

Or scout my charge: — He half desires my death;
But the despatch to Bouillon, some dark scheme
Against *his* crown — *there* is our weapon, Joseph;
With that, all safe — without it, all is peril!
Meanwhile to my old castle; *you* to court,
Diving with careless eyes into men's hearts,
As ghostly churchmen should do! See the King,
Bid him peruse that sage and holy treatise,
Wherein 'tis set forth how a Premier should
Be chosen from the Priesthood — how the King
Should never listen to a single charge
Against his servant, nor conceal one whisper
That the rank envies of a court distil
Into his ear — to fester the fair name
Of my — I mean his Minister! — Oh! Joseph,
A most convincing treatise.*

      Good — all favours,
If François be but bold, and Huguet honest.
Huguet — I half suspect — he bow'd too low —
'Tis not his way.
  Joseph. This is the curse, my Lord,
Of your high state; — suspicion of all men.
  Rich. [*sadly*]. True; — true; — my leeches bribed
   to poisoners; — pages
To strangle me in sleep. — My very King

---

* This tract, on the "Unity of the Minister," contains all the doctrines, and many more to the same effect, referred to in the text, and had a prodigious influence on the conscience of the poor King. At the onset of his career, Richelieu, as deputy of the clergy of Poitou, complained in his harangue to the King that ecclesiastics were too rarely summoned to the royal councils, and invoked the example of the Druids.

64   RICHELIEU;   [ACT II.

(This brain the unresting loom, from which was woven
The purple of his greatness) leagued against me.
Old — childless — friendless — broken — all forsake —
All — all — but —
 Joseph.   What?
 Rich.   The indomitable heart
Of Armand Richelieu!
 Joseph.   Nought beside?
 Rich.   Why, Julie,
My own dear foster-child, forgive me; — yes;
This morning, shining through their happy tears,
Thy soft eyes bless'd me! — and thy Lord, — in danger,
He would forsake me not.
 Joseph.   And Joseph ——
 Rich. [*after a pause.*]   You —
Yes, I believe you — yes — for all men fear you
And the world loves you not. And I, friend Joseph,
I am the only man who could, my Joseph,
Make you a Bishop.* Come, we'll go to dinner,
And talk the while of methods to advance
Our Mother Church.** Ah, Joseph, — *Bishop Joseph!*

---

 * Joseph's ambition was not, however, so moderate; he refused a bishopric, and desired the cardinal's hat, for which favour Richelieu openly supplicated the Holy See, but contrived somehow or other never to effect it, although two ambassadors applied for it at Rome.
 ** The peculiar religion of Père Joseph may be illustrated by the following anecdote: — An officer, whom he had dismissed upon an expedition into Germany, moved by conscience at the orders he had received, returned for further explanations, and found the Capuchin *disant sa messe.* He approached and whispered, "But, my father, if these people defend themselves —" "Kill all!" ("*Qu'on les tost*"), answered the good father, continuing his devotions.

ACT III.

SECOND DAY (MIDNIGHT).

SCENE I. — RICHELIEU's *Castle at Ruelle.* *A Gothic Chamber. Moonlight at the window, occasionally obscured.*

Rich. [*reading*].* "In silence, and at night, the Conscience feels
That life should soar to nobler ends than Power."
So sayest thou, sage and sober moralist!
But wert thou tried? Sublime Philosophy,
Thou art the Patriarch's ladder, reaching heav'en,
And bright with beck'ning angels — but, alas!
We see thee, like the Patriarch, but in dreams,
By the first step — dull-slumbering on the earth.
I am not happy! — with the Titan's lust
I woo'd a goddess, and I clasp a cloud.

---

* I need not say that the great length of this soliloquy adapts it only for the closet, and that but few of the lines are retained on the stage. To the reader, however, the passages omitted in representation will not, perhaps, be the most uninteresting in the play, and may be deemed necessary to the completion of the Cardinal's portrait, — action on the stage supplying so subtly the place of words in the closet. The self-assured sophistries which, in the text, mingle with Richelieu's better-founded arguments, in apology for the darker traits of his character, are to be found scattered throughout the writings ascribed to him. The reader will observe that in this self-confession lies the latent poetical justice, which separates happiness from success.

When I am dust, my name shall, like a star,
Shine through wan space, a glory — and a prophet
Whereby pale seers shall from their aëry towers
Con all the ominous signs, benign or evil,
That make the potent astrologue of kings.
But shall the Future judge me by the ends
That I have wrought — or by the dubious means
Through which the stream of my renown hath run
Into the many-voiced unfathom'd Time?
Foul in its bed lie weeds — and heaps of slime,
And with its waves — when sparkling in the sun,
Ofttimes the secret rivulets that swell
Its might of waters — blend the hues of blood.
Yet are my sins not those of CIRCUMSTANCE,
That all-pervading atmosphere, wherein
Our spirits, like the unsteady lizard, take
The tints that colour, and the food that nurtures?
* O! ye, whose hour-glass shifts its tranquil sands
In the unvex'd silence of a student's cell;
Ye, whose untempted hearts have never toss'd
Upon the dark and stormy tides where life
Gives battle to the elements, — and man
Wrestles with man for some slight plank, whose weight
Will bear but one — while round the desperate wretch
The hungry billows roar — and the fierce Fate,
Like some huge monster, dim-seen through the surf,
Waits him who drops; — ye safe and formal men,
Who write the deeds, and with unfeverish hand

* Retained in representation.

Weigh in nice scales the motives of the Great,
Ye cannot know what ye have never tried!
History preserves only the fleshless bones
Of what we are — and by the mocking skull
The would-be wise pretend to guess the features!
Without the roundness and the glow of life
How hideous is the skeleton! Without
The colourings and humanities that clothe
Our errors, the anatomists of schools
Can make our memory hideous!
                                I have wrought
Great uses out of evil tools — and they
In the time to come may bask beneath the light
Which I have stolen from the angry gods,
And warn their sons against the glorious theft,
Forgetful of the darkness which it broke.
I have shed blood — but I have had no foes
Save those the State had* — if my wrath was deadly,
'Tis that I felt my country in my veins,
And smote her sons as Brutus smote his own.**
And yet I am not happy — blanch'd and sear'd
Before my time — breathing an air of hate,
And seeing daggers in the eyes of men,
And wasting powers that shake the thrones of earth
In contest with the insects — bearding kings

---

* It is well known that when, on his death-bed, Richelieu was asked if he forgave his enemies; he replied, "I never had any, but those of the State." And this was true enough, for Richelieu and the State were one.

** Richelieu's vindication of himself from cruelty will be found in various parts of Petitot's Collection, vols. xxi. xxx. (bis).

And braved by lackies * — murder at my bed;
And lone amidst the multitudinous web,
With the dread Three — that are the Fates who hold
The woof and shears — the Monk, the Spy, the Headsman.
And this is power? Alas! I am not happy.
               [*After a pause.*
And yet the Nile is fretted by the weeds
Its rising roots not up; but never yet
Did one least barrier by a ripple vex
My onward tide, unswept in sport away.
Am I so ruthless then that I do hate
Them who hate me? Tush, tush! I do not hate;
Nay, I forgive. The Statesman writes the doom,
But the Priest sends the blessing. I forgive them,
But I destroy; forgiveness is mine own,
Destruction is the State's! For private life,
Scripture the guide — for public, Machiavel.
Would fortune serve me if the Heaven were wroth?
For chance makes half my greatness. I was born
Beneath the aspect of a bright-eyed star,

* Voltaire has a striking passage on the singular fate of Richelieu, recalled every hour from his gigantic schemes to frustrate some miserable cabal of the ante-room. Richelieu would often exclaim, that "Six pieds de terre," as he called the king's cabinet, "lui donnaient plus de peine que tout le reste de l'Europe." The death of Wallenstein, sacrificed by the Emperor Ferdinand, produced a most lively impression upon Richelieu. He found many traits of comparison between Ferdinand and Louis — Wallenstein and himself. In the Memoirs — now regarded by the best authorities as written by his sanction, and in great part by himself — the great Frenchman bursts (when alluding to Wallenstein's murder) into a touching and pathetic anathema on the *misère de cette vie* of dependence on jealous and timid royalty, which he himself, while he wrote, sustained. It is worthy of remark, that it was precisely at the period of Wallenstein's death that Richelieu obtained from the king an augmentation of his guard,

And my triumphant adamant of soul
Is but the fix'd persuasion of success.
Ah! — here! — that spasm! — again! — How Life
    and Death
Do wrestle for me momently! And yet
The King looks pale. I shall outlive the King!
And then, thou insolent Austrian — who didst gibe
At the ungainly, gaunt, and daring lover, *
Sleeking thy looks to silken Buckingham, —
Thou shalt — no matter! — I have outlived love.
O! beautiful — all golden — gentle youth!
Making thy palace in the careless front
And hopeful eye of man — ere yet the soul
Hath lost the memories which (so Plato dream'd)
Breathed glory from the earlier star it dwelt in —
Oh! for one gale from thine exulting morning,
Stirring amidst the roses, where of old
Love shook the dew-drops from his glancing hair!
Could I recall the past — or had not set
The prodigal treasures of the bankrupt soul
In one slight bark upon the shoreless sea;
The yoked steer, after his day of toil,
Forgets the goad, and rests — to me alike
Or day or night — Ambition has no rest!
Shall I resign? — who can resign himself?

---

* Richelieu was commonly supposed, though I cannot say I find much evidence for it, to have been too presuming in an interview with Anne of Austria (the Queen), and to have bitterly resented the contempt she expressed for him. The Duke of Buckingham's frantic and Quixotic passion for the Queen is well known.

For custom is ourself; as drink and food
Become our bone and flesh — the aliments
Nurturing our nobler part, the mind — thoughts, dreams,
Passions, and aims, in the revolving cycle
Of the great alchemy — at length are made
Our mind itself; and yet the sweets of leisure —
An honour'd home — far from those base intrigues —
An eyrie on the heaven-kiss'd heights of wisdom —
[*Taking up the book.*
Speak to me, moralist! — I'll heed thy counsel.
Were it not best —

Enter FRANÇOIS *hastily, and in part disguised.*

Rich. [*flinging away the book*]. Philosophy, thou liest!
Quick — the despatch! Power — Empire! Boy — the packet!

Fran. Kill me, my Lord.

Rich. They knew thee — they suspected —
They gave it not —

Fran. He gave it — *he* — the Count
De Baradas — with his own hand he gave it!

Rich. Baradas! Joy! out with it!

Fran. Listen,
And then dismiss me to the headsman.

Rich. Ha!
Go on.

Fran. They led me to a chamber — There
Orleans and Baradas, and some half-score,
Whom I know not — were met —

Rich. Not more!

Fran. But from
The adjoining chamber broke the din of voices,
The clattering tread of arm'd men; at times
A shriller cry, that yell'd out, "Death to Richelieu!"

Rich. Speak not of me: thy country is in danger!
The adjoining room — So, so — a *separate* treason!
The one thy ruin, France! — the meaner crime,
Left to their tools, my murder!

Fran. Baradas
Question'd me close — demurr'd — until, at last,
O'erruled by Orleans, — gave the packet — told me
That life and death were in the scroll — this gold —

Rich. Gold is no proof —

Fran. And Orleans promised thousands,
When Bouillon's trumpets in the streets of Paris
Rang out shrill answer. Hastening from the house,
My footstep in the stirrup, Marion stole
Across the threshold,.whispering, "Lose no moment
Ere Richelieu have the packet: tell him too —
Murder is in the winds of Night, and Orleans
Swears, ere the dawn the Cardinal shall be clay."
She said, and trembling fled within; when, lo!
A band of iron griped me; through the dark
Gleam'd the dim shadow of an arm'd man:
Ere I could draw — the prize was wrested from me,
And a hoarse voice gasp'd — "Spy, I spare thee, for
This steel is virgin to thy Lord!" with that
He vanish'd. — Scared and trembling for thy safety
I mounted, fled, and, kneeling at thy feet,

Implore thee to acquit my faith — but not,
Like him, to spare my life.
  Rich.   Who spake of *life?*
I bade thee grasp that treasure as thine *honour* —
A jewel worth whole hecatombs of lives!
Begone! — redeem thine honour — back to Marion —
Or Baradas — or Orleans — track the robber —
Regain the packet — or crawl on to Age —
Age and grey hairs like mine — and know, thou hast lost
That which had made thee great and saved thy country.—
See me not till thou'st bought the right to seek me. —
Away! — Nay, cheer thee, thou hast not fail'd yet, —
There's no such word as "fail!"
  Fran.   Bless you, my Lord,
For that one smile! — I'll wear it on my heart
To light me back to triumph.*   [*Exit.*
  Rich.   The poor youth!
An elder had ask'd life! — I love the young!
For as great men live not in their own time,
But the next race, — so in the young, my soul
Makes many Richelieus. He will win it yet.
François! — He's gone. My murder! Marion's warning!
This bravo's threat! Oh for the morrow's dawn!
I'll set my spies to work — I'll make all space

---

* The fear and the hatred which Richelieu generally inspired were not shared by his dependents and those about his person, who are said "to have adored him." — "Ses domestiques le regardaient comme le meilleur des maîtres." — *Le Clerc*. In fact, although "*il étoit orgueilleux et colère,*" — he was, "*en même temps, affable et plein de douceur dans l'abord;*" and he was no less generous to those who served than severe to those who opposed him.

(As does the sun) a Universal Eye —
Huguet shall track — Joseph confess — ha! ha!
Strange, while I laugh'd I shudder'd — and ev'n now
Through the chill air the beating of my heart
Sounds like a death-watch by a sick man's pillow;
If Huguet *could* deceive me — hoofs without —
The gates unclose — steps near and nearer!

Enter JULIE.

Julie.   Cardinal!
My father!   [*Falls at his feet.*
    Rich.   Julie at this hour! — and tears!
What ails thee?
    Julie.   I am safe; I am with thee! —
    Rich. Safe! why in all the storms of this wide world
What wind would mar the violet?
    Julie.   That man —
Why did I love him? — clinging to a breast
That knows no shelter?
                    Listen — late at noon —
The marriage-day — ev'n then no more a lover —
He left me coldly, — well, — I sought my chamber
To weep and wonder — but to hope and dream.
Sudden a mandate from the King — to attend
Forthwith his pleasure at the Louvre.
    Rich.   Ha!
You did obey the summons; and the King
Reproach'd your hasty nuptials.
    Julie.   Were that all!
He frown'd and chid; proclaim'd the bond unlawful:

Bade me not quit my chamber in the palace,
And there at night — alone — this night — all still —
He sought my presence — dared — thou read'st the heart,
Read mine! — I cannot speak it!
 Rich.   He a king, —
You — woman; well, — you yielded!
 Julie.   Cardinal —
Dare you say "yielded?" — Humbled and abash'd,
He from the chamber crept — this mighty Louis;
Crept like a baffled felon! — yielded! Ah!
More royalty in woman's honest heart
Than dwells within the crown'd majesty
And sceptred anger of a hundred kings!
Yielded! — Heavens! — yielded!
 Rich.   To my breast, — close — close!
The world would never need a Richelieu, if
Men — bearded, mail'd men — the Lords of Earth —
Resisted flattery, falsehood, avarice, pride,
As this poor child with the dove's innocent scorn
Her sex's tempters, Vanity and Power! —
He left you — well!
 Julie.   Then came a sharper trial!
At the King's suit the Count de Baradas
Sought me to soothe, to fawn, to flatter, while
On his smooth lip insult appear'd more hateful
For the false mask of pity: letting fall
Dark hints of treachery, with a world of sighs
That Heaven had granted to so base a Lord
The heart whose coldest friendship were to him
What Mexico to misers! Stung at last

By my disdain, the dim and glimmering sense
Of his cloak'd words broke into bolder light,
And THEN — ah! then, my haughty spirit fail'd me!
Then I was weak — wept — oh! such bitter tears!
For (turn thy face aside and let me whisper
The horror to thine ear) then did I learn
That he — that Adrien — that my husband — knew
The King's polluting suit, and deem'd it *honour!*
Then all the terrible and loathsome truth
Glared on me; — coldness — waywardness, reserve —
Mystery of looks — words — all unravell'd, — and
I saw the impostor, where I had loved the god!
    Rich. I think thou wrong'st thy husband — but
        proceed.
    Julie. Did you say "wrong'd" him? — Cardinal,
        my father,
Did you say "wrong'd?" Prove it, and life shall grow
One prayer for thy reward and his forgiveness.
    Rich. Let me know all.
    Julie.   To the despair he caused
The courtier left me; but amid the chaos
Darted one guiding ray — to 'scape — to fly —
Reach Adrien, learn the worst — 'twas then near
        midnight:
Trembling I left my chamber — sought the Queen —
Fell at her feet — reveal'd the unholy peril —
Implored her aid to flee our joint disgrace.
Moved, she embraced and soothed me; nay, preserved;
Her word sufficed to unlock the palace-gates:
I hasten'd home — but home was desolate, —

No Adrien there! Fearing the worst, I fled
To thee, directed hither. As my wheels
Paused at thy gates — the clang of arms behind —
The ring of hoofs —
    Rich.   'Twas but my guards, fair trembler.
(So Huguet keeps his word, my omens wrong'd him.)
    Julie. Oh, in one hour what years of anguish crowd!
    Rich. Nay, there's no danger now. Thou needest rest.
Come, thou shalt lodge beside me. Tush! be cheer'd.
My rosiest Amazon — thou wrong'st thy Theseus.
All will be well — yes, yet all well.
                 [*Exeunt through a side door.*

SCENE II.

Enter HUGUET — DE MAUPRAT, *in complete armour; his vizor down. The moonlight obscured at the casement.*

    Hug.   Not here!
    De Mau. Oh, I will find him, fear not. Hence and guard
The galleries where the menials sleep — plant sentries
At every outlet — Chance should throw no shadow
Between the vengeance and the victim! Go! —
Ere yon brief vapour that obscures the moon,
As doth our deed pale conscience, pass away,
The mighty shall be ashes.
    Hug.   Will you not
A second arm?

De Mau.   To slay one weak old man? —
Away! No lesser wrongs than mine can make
This murder lawful. Hence!
    Hug.   A short farewell!
                               [*Exit* HUGUET.

    Re-enter RICHELIEU [*not perceiving* DE MAUPRAT].

    Rich. How heavy is the air! — the vestal lamp
Of the sad Moon, weary with vigil, dies
In the still temple of the solemn heaven!
The very darkness lends itself to fear —
To treason ———
    De Mau.   And to death!
    Rich.   My omens lied not!
What art thou, wretch?
    De Mau.   Thy doomsman!
    Rich.   Ho, my guards!
Huguet! Montbrassil! Vermont!
    De Mau.   Ay, thy spirits
Forsake thee, wizard; thy bold men of mail
Are *my confederates.* Stir not! but one step,
And know the next — thy grave!
    Rich.   Thou liest, knave!
I am old, infirm — most feeble — but thou liest!
Armand de Richelieu dies not by the hand
Of man — the stars have said it* — and the voice

---

* In common with his contemporaries, Richelieu was credulous in astrology and less lawful arts. He was too fortunate a man not to be superstitious.

Of my own prophet and oracular soul
Confirms the shining Sibyls! Call them all
Thy brother butchers! Earth has no such fiend —
No! as one parricide of his father-land,
Who dares in Richelieu murder France!
  De Mau.   Thy stars
Deceive thee, Cardinal; thy soul of wiles
May against kings and armaments avail,
And mock the embattled world; but powerless now
Against the sword of one resolved man,
Upon whose forehead thou hast written shame!
  Rich. I breathe; he is not a hireling. Have I wrong'd
   thee?
Beware surmise — suspicion — lies! I am
Too great for men to speak the truth of me!
  De Mau. Thy *acts* are thy accusers, Cardinal!
In his hot youth, a soldier, urged to crime
Against the State, placed in your hands his life; —
You did not strike the blow — but o'er his head,
Upon the gossamer thread of your caprice,
Hover'd the axe. His the brave spirit's hell,
The twilight terror of suspense; — your death
Had set him free; he purposed not, nor pray'd it.
One day you summon'd — mock'd him with smooth
   pardon —
Shower'd wealth upon him —. bade an angel's face
Turn Earth to Paradise ——
  Rich.   Well!
  De Mau.   Was this mercy?
A Cæsar's generous vengeance? — Cardinal, no!

Judas, not Cæsar, was the model! You
Saved him from death for shame; reserved to grow
The scorn of living men — to his dead sires
Leprous reproach — scoff of the age to come —
A kind convenience — a Sir Pandarus
To his own bride, and the august adulterer!
Then did the first great law of human hearts,
Which with the patriot's, not the rebel's, name
Crown'd the first Brutus, when the Tarquin fell,
Make Misery royal — raise this desperate wretch
Into thy destiny! Expect no mercy!
Behold De Mauprat!   [*Lifts his vizor.*

   Rich.   To thy knees, and crawl
For pardon; or, I tell thee, thou shalt live
For such remorse, that, did I hate thee, I
Would bid thee strike, that I might be avenged!
It was to save my Julie from the King,
That in thy valour I forgave thy crime; —
It was, when thou — the rash and ready tool —
Yea, of that shame thou loath'st — didst leave thy hearth
To the polluter — in these arms thy bride
Found the protecting shelter thine withheld.
                              [*Goes to the side door.*
Julie de Mauprat — Julie!
              Enter JULIE.
                 Lo! my witness!

  De Mau. What marvel's this? — I dream! my Julie — *thou!*
This, thy beloved hand?

Julie.   Henceforth all bond
Between us twain is broken. Were it not
For this old man, I might, in truth, have lost
The right — now mine — to scorn thee!
   Rich.   So, you hear her?
   De Mau. Thou with some slander hast her sense
      infected!
   Julie. No, sir, he did excuse thee in despite
Of all that wears the face of truth. Thy *friend* —
Thy *confidant* — familiar — *Baradas* —
Himself reveal'd thy baseness.
   De Mau.   Baseness!
   Rich.   Ay;
That *thou didst court* dishonour.
   De Mau.   Baradas!
Where is thy thunder, Heaven? — Duped! — snared!
   — undone!
Thou — thou couldst not believe him! Thou dost
   love me!
Love cannot feed upon falsehoods!
   Julie [*aside*].   Love him! — Ah!
Be still, my heart! [*Aloud.*] Love you I did: — how
   fondly,
Woman — if women were my listeners now —
Alone could tell! — For ever fled my dream:
Farewell — all's over!
   Rich.   Nay, my daughter, these
Are but the blinding mists of day-break love
Sprung from its very light, and heralding
A noon of happy summer. — Take her hand

And speak the truth, with which your heart runs
    over —
That this Count Judas — this Incarnate Falsehood —
Never lied more, than when he told thy Julie
That Adrien loved her not — except, indeed,
When he told Adrien, Julie could betray him.
    Julie [*embracing* DE MAUPRAT]. You love me, then!
    — you love me! and they wrong'd you!
    De Mau. Ah! couldst thou doubt it?
    Rich.   Why, the very mole
Less blind than thou! Baradas loves thy wife; —
Had hoped her hand — aspired to be that cloak
To the King's will, which to thy bluntness seems
The Centaur's poisonous robe — hopes even now
To make thy corpse his footstool to thy bed!
Where was thy wit, man? — Ho! these schemes are
    glass!
The very sun shines through them.
    De Mau.   O, my Lord.
Can you forgive me?
    Rich.   Ay, and save you!
    De Mau.   Save! —
Terrible word! — O, save *thyself;* — these halls
Swarm with thy foes: already for thy blood
Pants thirsty Murder!
    Julie.   Murder!
    Rich.   Hush! put by
The woman. Hush! a shriek — a cry — a breath
Too loud, would startle from its horrent pause

The swooping Death! Go to the door, and listen! —
Now for escape!
  De Mau. None — none! Their blades shall pass
This heart to thine.
  Rich. [*drily*]. An honourable outwork
But much too near the citadel. I think
That I can trust you now [*slowly, and gazing on him*]:
   — yes; I can trust you.
How many of my troop league with you?
  De Mau.   All! —
We *are* your troop!
  Rich.   And Huguet?
  De Mau.   Is our captain.
  Rich. A retributive Power! — This comes, of spies!
All? then the lion's skin's too short to-night, —
Now for the fox's! —
  Julie.   A hoarse, gathering murmur! —
Hurrying and heavy footsteps!
  Rich.   Ha! — the posterns?
  De Mau. No egress where no sentry!
  Rich.   Follow me —
I have it! — to my chamber — quick! Come, Julie!
Hush! Mauprat, come!
  [*Murmur at a distance.*] — Death to the Cardinal!
  Rich. Bloodhounds, I laugh at ye! — ha! ha! —
   we will
Baffle them yet. — Ha! — ha!
     [*Exeunt* JULIE, MAUPRAT, RICHELIEU.
  Hug. [*without*].   This way — this way!

SCENE III.

Enter HUGUET *and the* Conspirators.

Hug. De Mauprat's hand is never slow in battle; —
Strange, if it falter now! Ha! gone!

First Con.   Perchance
The fox had crept to rest; and to his lair
Death, the dark hunter, tracks him.

[*Enter* MAUPRAT, *throwing open the doors of the recess, in which a bed, whereon* RICHELIEU *lies extended.*

De Mau.   Live the King!
Richelieu is dead!

Hug. [*advancing towards the recess;* MAUPRAT *following, his hand on his dagger*]. Are his eyes open?

De Mau.   Ay,
As if in life!

Hug. [*turning back*]. I will not look on him.
You have been long.

De Mau.   I watch'd him till he slept.
Heed me. — No trace of blood reveals the deed; —
Strangled in sleep. His health hath long been broken —
Found breathless in his bed. So runs our tale,
Remember! Back to Paris — Orleans gives
Ten thousand crowns, and Baradas a lordship,
To him who first gluts vengeance with the news
That Richelieu is in heaven! Quick, that all France
May share your joy!

Hug. And you?
De Mau. Will stay, to crush
Eager suspicion — to forbid sharp eyes
To dwell too closely on the clay; prepare
The rites, and place him on his bier — this *my* task.
I leave to you, sirs, the more grateful lot
Of wealth and honours. Hence!
Hug. I shall be noble!
De Mau. Away!
First Con. Five thousand crowns!
Omnes. To horse! — to horse! [*Exeunt* Conspirators.

SCENE IV.

Still night — A room in the house of COUNT DE BARADAS, *lighted, &c.*

ORLEANS *and* DE BERINGHEN.

De Ber. I understand. Mauprat kept guard without:
Knows nought of the despatch — but heads the troop
Whom the poor Cardinal fancies his protectors.
Save us from such protection!
Orle. Yet, if Huguet,
By whose advice and proffers we renounced
Our earlier scheme, should still be Richelieu's minion,
And play us false —
De Ber. The fox must then devour
The geese he gripes (I'm out of it, thank Heaven!)
And you must swear you smelt the trick, but seem'd
To approve the deed — to render up the doers.

Enter BARADAS.

Bar. Julie is fled: — the King, whom now I left
To a most thorny pillow, vows revenge
On her — on Mauprat — and on Richelieu! Well;
We loyal men anticipate his wish
Upon the last — and as for Mauprat, —' [*Showing a writ.*

De Ber.   Hum!
They say the devil invented printing! Faith,
He has some hand in writing parchment — eh, Count?
What mischief now?
    Bar.   The King, at Julie's flight
Enraged, will brook no rival in a subject —
So on this old offence — the affair of Faviaux —
Ere Mauprat can tell tales of *us*, we build
His bridge between the dungeon and the grave.
    Orle. Well; if our courier can but reach the army,
The cards are ours! — and yet, I own, I tremble.
Our names are in the scroll — discovery, death!
    Bar. Success, a crown!
    De Ber. [*apart to* BARADAS]. Our future Regent is
No hero.
    Bar. [to DE BERINGHEN]. But his rank makes others valiant;
And on his cowardice I mount to power.
Were Orleans Regent — what were Baradas?
Oh! by the way — I had forgot, your Highness,
Friend Huguet whisper'd me, "Beware of Marion:
I've seen her lurking near the Cardinal's palace."
Upon that hint, I've found her lodging elsewhere.

Orle. You wrong her, Count. Poor Marion!—she adores me.

Bar. [*apologetically*]. Forgive me, but —

Enter Page.

Page. My Lord, a rude, strange soldier, Breathless with haste, demands an audience.

Bar. So! — The archers?

Page. In the ante-room, my Lord, As you desired.

Bar. 'Tis well — admit the soldier.

[*Exit* Page.

Huguet! — I bade him seek me here.

Enter HUGUET.

Hug. My Lords. The deed is done. Now, Count, fulfil your word, And make me noble!

Bar. Richelieu dead? — art sure? How died he?

Hug. Strangled in his sleep: — no blood, No tell-tale violence.

Bar. Strangled? — monstrous villain! Reward for murder! Ho, there! [*Stamping.*

Enter Captain *with five* Archers.

Hug. No, thou durst not!

Bar. Seize on the ruffian — bind him — gag him! Off To the Bastile!

Hug.   Your word — your plighted faith!
Bar. Insolent liar! ho, away!
Hug.   Nay, Count;
I have that about me, which —
Bar.   Away with him!
            [*Exeunt* HUGUET *and* Archers.
Now, then, all's safe; Huguet must die in prison,
So Mauprat: — coax or force the meaner crew
To fly the country. Ha, ha! thus, your highness,
Great men make use of little men.
    De Ber.   My Lords,
Since our suspense is ended — you'll excuse me;
'Tis late — and, *entre nous*, I have not supp'd yet!
I'm one of the new Council now, remember;
I feel the public stirring here already;
A very craving monster. *Au revoir!*
                    [*Exit* DE BERINGHEN.
    Orle. No fear, now Richelieu's dead.
    Bar.   And could he come
To life again, he could not keep life's life —
His power, — nor save De Mauprat from the scaffold, —
Nor Julie from these arms — nor Paris from
The Spaniard — nor your highness from the throne!
All ours! all ours! in spite of my Lord Cardinal!

            Enter Page.
    Page. A gentleman, my Lord, of better mien
Than he who last —
    Bar.   Well, he may enter.
                        [*Exit* Page.

Orle.   Who
Can this be?
   Bar.   One of the conspirators:
Mauprat himself, perhaps.

              Enter FRANÇOIS.

   Fran.   My Lord —
   Bar.   Ha, traitor!
In Paris still?
   Fran.   The packet — the despatch —
Some knave play'd spy without, and reft it from me,
Ere I could draw my sword.
   Bar.   Play'd spy *without!*
Did he wear armour?
   Fran.   Ay, from head to heel.
   Orle. One of our band. Oh, Heavens!
   Bar.   Could it be Mauprat?
Kept guard at the *door* — knew *nought of the despatch* —
How HE? — and yet, who other?
   Fran.   · Ha, De Mauprat!
The night was dark — his vizor closed.
   Bar.   'Twas he!
How could he guess? — 'sdeath! if he should betray us.
His hate to Richelieu dies with Richelieu — and
He was not great enough for treason. Hence!
Find Mauprat — beg, steal, filch, or force it back,
Or, as I live, the halter —

Fran.   By the morrow
I will regain it [*aside*], and redeem my honour!
                                      [*Exit* FRANÇOIS.
    Orle. Oh, we are lost —
    Bar.   Not so! But cause on cause
For Mauprat's seizure — silence — death! Take
       courage.
    Orle. Should it once reach the King, the Cardinal's
       arm
Could smite us from the grave.
    Bar.   Sir, think it not!
I hold De Mauprat in my grasp. To-morrow,
And France is ours! Thou dark and fallen Angel,
Whose name on earth's AMBITION — thou that mak'st
Thy throne on treasons, stratagems, and murder, —
And with thy fierce and blood-red smile canst quench
The guiding stars of solemn empire — hear us
(For we are thine) — and light us to the goal!

ACT IV.

THIRD DAY.

SCENE I. — *The Gardens of the Louvre.* — ORLEANS, BARADAS, DE BERINGHEN, Courtiers, &c.

    Orle. How does my brother bear the Cardinal's death?
    Bar. With grief, when thinking of the toils of State;
With joy, when thinking on the eyes of Julie; —
At times he sighs, "Who now shall govern France?"
Anon exclaims — "Who now shall baffle Louis?"
    Enter LOUIS *and other* Courtiers. [*They uncover.*]
    Orle. Now, my liege, now, I can embrace a brother.
    Louis. Dear Gaston, yes. — I do believe you *love* me; —
Richelieu denied it — sever'd us too long.
A great man, Gaston! Who shall govern France?
    Bar. Yourself, my liege. That swart and potent star
Eclipsed your royal orb. He served the country,
But did he *serve,* or seek to *sway* the *King?*
    [*Louis.* You're right — he was an able politician —
That's all: — between ourselves, Count, I suspect

The largeness of his learning — specially
In falcons* — a poor huntsman, too!
  Bar.   Ha — ha!
Your Majesty remembers —
  Louis.   Ay, the blunder
Between the *greffier* and the *souillard* when —
       [*Checks and crosses himself.*
Alas! poor sinners that we are! we laugh
While this great man — a priest, a cardinal,
A faithful servant — out upon us! —
  Bar.   Sire,
If my brow wear no cloud, 'tis that the Cardinal
No longer shades the King.
  Louis [*looking up at the skies*]. Oh, Baradas!
Am I not to be pitied? — what a day
For —
  Bar. Sorrow? — No, sire!

---

* Louis XIII. is said to have possessed some natural talents, and in earlier youth to have exhibited the germs of noble qualities; but a blight seems to have passed over his maturer life. Personally brave, but morally timid, — always governed, whether by his mother or his minister, and always repining at the yoke. The only affection amounting to a passion that he betrayed was for the sports of the field; yet it was his craving weakness (and this throws a kind of false interest over his character) to wish to be loved. He himself loved no one. He suffered the only woman who seems to have been attached to him to wither in a convent; — he gave up favourite after favourite to exile or the block. When Richelieu died, he said coldly, "Voilà un grand politique mort!" and when the ill-fated but unprincipled Cinq Mars, whom he called "*le cher ami,*" was beheaded, he drew out his watch at the fatal hour, and said with a smile, "I think at this moment that *le cher ami fait une vilaine mine.*" Nevertheless, his conscience at times (for he was devout and superstitious) made him gentle, and his pride and honour would often, when least expected, rouse him into haughty but brief resistance to the despotism under which he lived.

Louis.   Bah! for *hunting*, man,
And Richelieu's dead; 'twould be an indecorum
Till he is buried — [*yawns*] — life is very tedious.
I made a madrigal on life last week:
You do not sing,* Count? — Pity; you should learn.
Poor Richelieu had no ear — yet a great man.
Ah! what a weary weight devolves upon me!
These endless wars — these thankless Parliaments —
The snares in which he tangled States and Kings,
Like the old fisher of the fable, Proteus,
Netting great Neptune's wariest tribes, and changing
Into all shapes when Craft pursued himself:
Oh, a great man!
    Bar.   Your royal mother said so,
And died in exile.
    Louis [*sadly*]. True: I loved my mother.**
    Bar. The Cardinal dies. — Yet day revives the
            earth;
The rivers run not back. In truth, my liege,
Did your high orb on others shine as him,
Why, things as dull in their own selves as I am
Would glow as brightly with the borrow'd beam. ***

---

* Louis had some musical taste and accomplishment, wherewith he often communicated to his favourites some of that wearisome *ennui* under which he himself almost unceasingly languished.

** One of Louis's most bitter complaints against Richelieu was the continued banishment of the Queen Mother. It is impossible, however, not to be convinced that the return of that most worthless intriguante was wholly incompatible with the tranquillity of the kingdom. Yet, on the other hand, the poverty and privation which she endured in exile are discreditable to the generosity and the gratitude of Richelieu; she was his first patron, though afterwards his most powerful persecutor.

*** In his Memoirs, Richelieu gives an amusing account of the in-

Louis. Ahem! — He was too stern.
Orle. A very Nero.
Bar. His power was like the Capitol of old —
Built on a human skull.
Louis. And, had he lived,
I know another head, my Baradas,
That would have propp'd the pile: I've seen him eye
    thee
With a most hungry fancy.
Bar. [*anxiously*]. Sire, I knew
You would protect me.
Louis. Did you so? of course!
And yet he had a way with him — a something
That always — But no matter — he is dead.
And, after all, men call his King "The Just," *
And so I am. Dear Count, this silliest Julie,
I know not why, she takes my fancy. Many
As fair, and certainly more kind; but yet
It is so. Count, I am no lustful Tarquin,
And do abhor the bold and frontless vices

---

solence and arts of Baradas, and observes, with indignant astonishment, that the favourite was never weary of repeating to the King that he (Baradas) would have made just as great a minister as Richelieu. It is on the attachment of Baradas to La Cressias, a maid of honour to the Queen Mother, of whom, according to Baradas, the King was enamoured also, that his love for the Julie de Mortemar of the play has been founded. The secret of Baradas's sudden and extraordinary influence with the King seems to rest in the personal adoration which he professed for Louis, with whom he affected all the jealousy of a lover, but whom he flattered with the ardent chivalry of a knight. Even after his disgrace he placed upon his banner, "Fiat voluntas tua."

* Louis was called The Just, but for no other reason than that he was born under the Libra.

Which the Church justly censures; yet, 'tis sad
On rainy days to drag out weary hours * —
Deaf to the music of a woman's voice —
Blind to the sunshine of a woman's eyes.
It is no sin in Kings to seek amusement;
And that is all I seek. I miss her much —
She has a silver laugh — a rare perfection.
   Bar. Richelieu was most disloyal in that marriage.]
   Louis [*querulously*]. He knew that Julie pleased me:
      — a clear proof
He never loved me!
   Bar.   Oh, most clear! — But now
No bar between the Lady and your will!
This writ makes all secure: a week or two
In the Bastile will sober Mauprat's love,
And leave him eager to dissolve a hymen
That brings him such a home.
   Louis.   See to it, Count,
                               [*Exit* BARADAS.
I'll summon Julie back. A word with you.
      [*Takes aside* First Courtier, *and* DE BERINGHEN, *and
      passes, conversing with them, through the Gardens.*

                Enter FRANÇOIS.
   Fran. All search, as yet, in vain for Mauprat! —
      Not
At home since yesternoon — a soldier told me

---

* Louis XIII. did not resemble either his father or his son in the ardour of his attachments; if not wholly platonic, they were wholly unimpassioned: yet no man was more jealous, or more unscrupulously tyrannical when the jealousy was aroused.

He saw him pass this way with hasty strides;
Should he meet Baradas — they'd rend it from him —
And then — benignant Fortune smiles upon me —
I am thy son! — if thou desert'st me now,
Come, Death, and snatch me from disgrace. But, no,
There's a great Spirit ever in the air
That from prolific and far-spreading wings
Scatters the seeds of honour — yea, the walls
And moats of castled forts — the barren seas —
The cell wherein the pale-eyed student holds
Talk with melodious science — all are sown
With everlasting honours, if our souls
Will toil for fame as boors for bread —

Enter MAUPRAT.

De Mau. Oh, let me—
Let me but meet him foot to foot — I'll dig
The Judas from his heart; — albeit the King
Should o'er him cast the purple!
    Fran. Mauprat! hold: —
Where is the —
    De Mau. Well! What wouldst thou?
    Fran. The despatch!
The packet — Look ON ME — I serve the Cardinal —
You know me. — Did you not keep guard last night
By Marion's house?
    De Mau. I did; — no matter now!
They told me *he* was *here!* —
    Fran. O joy! quick — quick —
The packet thou didst wrest from me!

De Mau. The packet?
What, art thou he I deem'd the Cardinal's spy
(Dupe that I was) — and overhearing Marion —
Fran. The same — restore it! haste!
De Mau. I have it not:
Methought it but reveal'd our scheme to Richelieu,
And, as we mounted, gave it to —

Enter BARADAS.
Stand back!
Now, villain! now — I have thee!
[*To* FRANÇOIS]. Hence, sir! — *Draw!*
Fran. Art mad? — the King's at hand! leave *him*
to Richelieu!
Speak — the despatch — to whom —
De Mau. [*dashing him aside, and rushing to* BARADAS].
Thou triple slanderer!
I'll set my heel upon thy crest! [*A few passes.*
Fran. Fly — fly! —
The King!

Enter at one side LOUIS, ORLEANS, DE BERINGHEN, *Courtiers, &c.; at the other, the* Guards *hastily.*
Louis. Swords drawn — before our very palace!
Have our laws died with Richelieu?
Bar. Pardon, Sire, —
My crime but self-defence.* [*Aside to* King.] It is De
Mauprat!

* One of Richelieu's severest and least politic laws was that which made duelling a capital crime. Never was the punishment against the

Louis. Dare he thus brave us?

[BARADAS *goes to the* Guard, *and gives the writ.*

De Mau. Sire, in the Cardinal's name —
Bar. Seize him — disarm — to the Bastile!

[DE MAUPRAT *seized, struggles with the* Guard — FRAN-
ÇOIS *restlessly endeavouring to pacify and speak to
him — when the gates open. Enter* RICHELIEU —
JOSEPH — *followed by* Arquebusiers.

Bar. The Dead Return'd to life!

Louis. What a *mock* death! this tops The Infinite of Insult.

De Mau. [*breaking from the* Guards]. Priest and Hero! —
For you are both — protect the truth!

Rich. [*taking the writ from the* Guard]. What's this?

De Ber. Fact in Philosophy. Foxes have got Nine lives, as well as cats!

Bar. Be firm, my liege.

Louis. I have assumed the sceptre — I will wield it!

Joseph. The tide runs counter — there'll be ship-
wreck somewhere.

[BARADAS *and* ORLEANS *keep close to the King, whispering and prompting him when* RICHELIEU *speaks.*

---

offence more relentlessly enforced; and never were duels so desperate and so numerous. The punishment of death must be evidently ineffectual so long as to refuse a duel is to be dishonoured, and so long as men hold the doctrine, however wrong, that it is better to part with the life that Heaven gave than the honour man makes. In fact, the greater the danger he incurred, the greater was the punctillio of the cavalier of that time in braving it.

Rich. High treason — Faviaux! still that stale
    pretence!
My liege, bad men (ay, Count, most *knavish* men!)
Abuse your royal goodness. For this soldier,
France hath none braver — and his youth's hot folly,
Misled — (by whom *your Highness* may conjecture!) —
Is long since cancell'd by a loyal manhood. —
I, Sire, have pardon'd him.
    Louis. And we do give
Your pardon to the winds. Sir, do your duty!
    Rich. What, Sire? — you do not know — Oh, par-
    don me —
You know not yet, that this brave, honest heart,
Stood between mine and murder! — Sire! for my
    sake —
For your old servant's sake — undo this wrong.
See, let me rend the sentence.
    Louis. At your peril!
This is too much: — Again, sir, do your duty!
    Rich. Speak not, but go: — I would not see young
    Valour
So humbled as grey Service.
    De Mau. Fare you well!
Save Julie, and console her.
    Fran. [*aside to* MAUPRAT]. The despatch!
Your fate, foes, life, hang on a word! — to whom?
    De Mau. To Huguet.
    Fran. Hush — keep counsel! —
    silence — hope!
        [*Exeunt* MAUPRAT *and* Guard.

Bar. [*aside* to FRANÇOIS]. Has he the packet?
Fran. He will not reveal —
[*Aside.*] Work, brain! — beat, heart! — "*There's no such word as fail!*" [*Exit* FRANÇOIS.
Rich. [*fiercely*]. Room, my Lords, room! — the Minister of France
Can need no intercession with the King.
[*They fall back.*
Louis. What means this false report of death, Lord Cardinal?
Rich. Are you then anger'd, Sire, that I live still?
Louis. No; but such artifice —
Rich. Not mine: — look elsewhere!
Louis — my castle swarm'd with the assassins.
Bar. [*advancing*]. We have punish'd them already. Huguet now
In the Bastile. — Oh! my Lord, *we* were prompt
To avenge you — *we* were —
Rich. WE? — Ha, ha! you hear,
My liege! What page, man, in the last court grammar
Made you a plural? Count, you have seized the
   hireling: —
Sire, shall I name the *master?*
Louis. Tush, my Lord,
The old contrivance: — ever does your wit
Invent assassins, — that ambition may
Slay rivals —
Rich. Rivals, Sire, in what?
Service to France? *I have none!* Lives the man

Whom Europe, paled before your glory, deems
Rival to Armand Richelieu?
    Louis.   What, so haughty!
Remember, he who made, can unmake.
    Rich.   Never!
Never! Your anger can recall your trust,
Annul my office, spoil me of my lands,
Rifle my coffers, — but my name — my deeds,
Are royal in a land beyond your sceptre!
Pass sentence on me, if you will; from Kings,
Lo! I appeal to time! [Be just, my liege —
I found your kingdom rent with heresies
And bristling with rebellion; lawless nobles
And breadless serfs; England fomenting discord;
Austria — her clutch on your dominion; Spain
Forging the prodigal gold of either Ind
To arm'd thunderbolts. The Arts lay dead,
Trade rotted in your marts, your Armies mutinous,
Your Treasury bankrupt. Would you now revoke
Your trust, so be it! and I leave you, sole
Supremest Monarch of the mightiest realm,
From Ganges to the Icebergs: — Look without;
No foe not humbled! — Look within; the Arts
Quit for your schools — their old Hesperides
The golden Italy! while through the veins
Of your vast empire flows in strengthening tides
TRADE, the calm health of nations!
                                      Sire, I know
Your smoother courtiers please you best — nor measure
Myself with them, — yet sometimes I would doubt

If Statesmen rock'd and dandled into power
Could leave such legacies to kings!
        [LOUIS *appears irresolute.*
 Bar. [*passing him, whispers*]. But Julie,
Shall I not summon her to court?]
 Louis [*motions to* BARADAS, *and turns haughtily to
  the* Cardinal]. Enough!
Your Eminence must excuse a longer audience.
To your own palace: — For our conference, this
Nor place — nor season.
 Rich.   Good my liege, for *Justice*
All place a temple, and all season, summer! —
Do you deny me justice? — Saints of Heaven!
He turns from me! — *Do you deny me justice?*
For fifteen years, while in these hands dwelt Empire,
The humblest craftsman — the obscurest vassal —
The very leper shrinking from the sun,
Though loathed by Charity, might ask for justice! —
Not with the fawning tone and crawling mien
Of some I see around you — Counts and Princes —
Kneeling for *favours;* — but, erect and loud,
As men who ask man's rights! — my liege, my Louis,
Do you refuse me justice — audience even —
In the pale presence of the baffled Murther?*
 Louis. Lord Cardinal — one by one you have
  sever'd from me
The bonds of human love. All near and dear

---

* For the haughty and rebuking tone which Richelieu assumed in his expostulations with the King, see his Memoirs (*passim*) in Petitot's collection, vols. 22-30 (*his*). Montesquieu, in one of his brilliant antitheses, says well of Richelieu, "Ill avila le roi, mais il illustra le règne."

Mark'd out for vengeance — exile or the scaffold.
You find me now amidst my trustiest friends,
My closest kindred; — you would tear them from me;
They murder *you* forsooth, since *me* they love!
Eno' of plots and treasons for one reign!
Home! — Home! and sleep away these phantoms!
  Rich.   Sire!
I — patience, Heaven! — sweet Heaven! Sire, from
   the foot
Of that Great Throne, these hands have raised aloft
On an Olympus, looking down on mortals
And worshipp'd by their awe — before the foot
Of that high throne, — spurn you the grey-hair'd man,
Who gave you empire — and now sues for safety?
  Louis. No: — when we see your Eminence in truth
At the *foot* of the throne — we'll listen to you.
            [*Exit* LOUIS.
  Orle.   Saved!
  Bar. For this deep thanks to Julie and to Mauprat!
  Rich. My Lord de Baradas — I pray your pardon —
You are to be my successor! — your hand, sir!
  Bar. [*aside*]. What can this mean?
  Rich.   It trembles, see! it trembles!
The hand that holds the destinies of nations
Ought to shake less! — poor Baradas — poor France!
  Bar. Insolent —
       [*Exeunt* BARADAS *and* ORLEANS.

SCENE II.

Rich. Joseph — Did you hear the King?
Joseph. I did — there's danger! Had you been less
    haughty* —
Rich. And suffer'd slaves to chuckle — "See the
    Cardinal —
How meek his Eminence is to-day" — I tell thee
This is a strife in which the loftiest look
Is the most subtle armour —
    Joseph.   But —
    Rich.   No time
For ifs and buts. I will accuse these traitors!
François shall witness that De Baradas
Gave him the secret missive for De Bouillon,
And told him life and death were in the scroll.
I will — I will —
    Joseph.   Tush! François is your creature;
So they will say, and laugh at you! — *your witness
Must be that same Despatch.*
    Rich.   Away to Marion!

---

* However "*orgueilleux*" and "*colère*" in his disputes with Louis, the Cardinal did not always disdain recourse to the arts of the courtier; once, after an angry discussion with the King, in which, as usual, Richelieu got the better, Louis, as they quitted the palace together, said, rudely, "Sortez le premier; vous êtes bien le roi de France." "Si je passe le premier," replied the minister, after a moment's hesitation, and with great adroitness, "ce ne peut être que comme le plus humble de vos serviteurs;" and he took a flambeau from one of the pages to light the King as he walked before him — "en reculant et sans tourner le dos."

Joseph. I have been there — she is seized — removed — imprison'd —
By the Count's orders.
    Rich.   Goddess of bright dreams,
My country — shalt thou lose me now, when most
Thou need'st thy worshipper? My native land!
Let me but ward this dagger from thy heart,
And die — but on thy bosom!

            Enter JULIE.
    Julie.   Heaven! I thank thee!
It cannot be, or this all-powerful man
Would not stand idly thus.
    Rich.   What dost *thou* here?
Home!
    Julie. Home! — is *Adrien there?* — you're dumb — yet strive
For words; I see them trembling on your lip,
But choked by pity. It *was* truth — all truth!
Seized — the Bastile — and in your presence, too
Cardinal, where is Adrien? — Think — he saved
Your life; — your name is infamy, if wrong
Should come to his!
    Rich.   Be soothed, child.
    Julie.   Child no more;
I love, and I am woman! Hope and suffer —
Love, suffering, hope, — what else doth make the strength
And majesty of woman? — Where is Adrien?

Rich. [*to* JOSEPH]. Your youth was never young —
   you never loved: —
Speak to her —

Joseph. Nay, take heed — the King's command,
'Tis true — I mean — the —

Julie [*to* RICHELIEU]. Let thine eyes meet mine;
Answer me but one word — I am a wife —
I ask thee for my *home* — my FATE — my ALL!
Where is my *husband?*

Rich. You are Richelieu's ward,
A soldier's bride: they who insist on truth
Must out-face fear; — you ask me for your husband?
There — where the clouds of Heaven look darkest, o'er
The domes of the Bastile!

Julie. I thank you, father;
You see I do not shudder. Heaven forgive you
The sin of this desertion!

Rich. [*detaining her*]. Whither wouldst thou?

Julie. Stay me not. Fie! I should be there already.
I am thy ward, and haply he may think
Thou'st taught *me* also to forsake the wretched!

Rich. I've fill'd those cells — with many — traitors all,
Had *they* wives too? — Thy memories, Power, are
   solemn!
Poor sufferer! — think'st thou that yon gates of woe
Unbar to love? Alas! if love once enter,
'Tis for the last farewell; between those walls

And the mute grave* — the blessed household sounds
Only heard once — while hungering at the door,
The headsman whets the axe.
  Julie.   O, mercy! mercy!
Save him, restore him, father! Art thou not
The Cardinal-King? — the Lord of life and death —
Beneath whose light, as deeps beneath the moon,
The solemn tides of Empire ebb and flow?
Art thou not Richelieu?
  Rich.   Yesterday I was! —
To-day, a very weak old man! — To-morrow,
I know not what!
  Julie. Do you conceive his meaning?
Alas! I cannot. But, methinks, my senses
Are duller than they were!
  Joseph.   The King is chafed
Against his servant. Lady, while we speak,
The lackey of the ante-room is not
More powerless than the Minister of France.
  [*Rich.* And yet the air is still; Heaven wears no cloud,
From Nature's silent orbit starts no portent
To warn the unconscious world; albeit this night
May with a morrow teem which, in my fall,
Would carry earthquake to remotest lands,
And change the Christian globe. What wouldst thou,
   woman?
Thy fate and his, with mine, for good or ill,

---

* "Selon l'usage de Louis XIII., faire arrêter quelqu'un pour crime d'état, et le faire mourir, l'était à peu près la même chose." — *Le Clerc.*

Are woven threads. In my vast sum of life
Millions such units merge.]

Enter First Courtier.

   First Cour.   Madame de Mauprat!
Pardon, your Eminence — even now I seek
This lady's home — commanded by the King
To pray her presence.
   Julie [*clinging to* RICHELIEU]. Think of my dead
        father! —
Think, how, an infant, clinging to your knees,
And looking to your eyes, the wrinkled care
Fled from your brow before the smile of childhood,
Fresh from the dews of Heaven! Think of this,
And take me to your breast.
   Rich.   To those who sent you! —
And say you found the virtue they would slay
Here — couch'd upon this heart, as at an altar,
And shelter'd by the wings of sacred Rome!
Begone!
   First Cour. My Lord, I am your friend and
        servant —
Misjudge me not; but never yet was Louis
So roused against you: — shall I take this answer? —
It were to be your foe.
   Rich.   All time my foe,
If I, a Priest, could cast this holy Sorrow
Forth from her last asylum!
   First Cour.   He is lost! [*Exit* First Courtier.

Rich.   God help thee, child! — she hears not! Look
          upon her!
The storm, that rends the oak, uproots the flower.
Her father loved me so! and in that age
When friends are brothers! She has been to me
Soother, nurse, plaything, daughter. Are these tears?*
Oh! shame, shame! — dotage!
Joseph.   Tears are not for eyes
That rather need the lightning, which can pierce
Through barrèd gates and triple walls, to smite
Crime, where it cowers in secret! — The Despatch!
Set every spy to work; — the morrow's sun
Must see that written treason in your hands,
Or rise upon your ruin.
Rich.   Ay — and close
Upon my corpse! — I am not made to live --
Friends, glory, France, all reft from me; — my star
Like some vain holiday mimicry of fire,
Piercing imperial Heaven, and falling down
Rayless and blacken'd, to the dust — a thing
For all men's feet to trample! Yea! — to-morrow
Triumph or death! Look up, child! — Lead us, Joseph.

[*As they are going out, enter* BARADAS *and* DE BERINGHEN.

---

* Like Cromwell and Rienzi, Richelieu appears to have been easily moved to tears. The Queen Mother, who put the hardest interpretation on that humane weakness, which is natural with very excitable temperaments, said that "il pleurait quand il voulait." I may add, to those who may be inclined to imagine that Richelieu appears in parts of this scene too dejected for consistency with so imperious a character, that it is recorded of him that "quand ses affaires ne réuississoient pas, il se trouvoit abattu et epouvanté, et quand il obtenoit ce qu'il souhaitoit, il étoit fier et insultant."

Bar. My Lord, the King cannot believe your Eminence
So far forgets your duty, and his greatness,
As to resist his mandate! Pray you, Madam,
Obey the King — no cause for fear!
    Julie.   My father!
    Rich. She shall not stir!
    Bar.   You are not of her kindred —
An orphan —
    Rich.   And her country is her mother!
    Bar. The country is the King!
    Rich.   Ay, is it so? —
Then wakes the power which in the age of iron
Burst forth to curb the great, and raise the low.
Mark, where she stands! — around her form I draw
The awful circle of our solemn church!
Set but a foot within that holy ground,
And on thy head — yea, though it wore a crown —
I launch the curse of Rome!
    Bar.   I dare not brave you!
I do but speak the orders of my King,
The church, your rank, power, very word, my Lord,
Suffice you for resistance: — blame yourself,
If it should cost you power!
    Rich.   That *my* stake. — Ah!
Dark gamester! *what is thine?* Look to it well! —
Lose not a trick. — By this same hour to-morrow
Thou shalt have France, or I thy head!
    Bar. [*aside to* De Beringhen].   He cannot
Have the Despatch?

De Ber. No: were it so, your stake
Were lost already.
  Joseph [*aside*]. Patience is your game:
Reflect, you have not the Despatch!
  Rich. O! monk!
Leave patience to the saints — for *I* am human!
Did not thy father die for France, poor orphan?
And now they say thou hast *no* father! — Fie!
Art thou not pure and good? — if so, thou art
A part of that — the Beautiful, the Sacred —
Which, in all climes, men that have hearts adore,
By the great title of their mother country!
  Bar. [*aside*]. He wanders!
  Rich. So cling close unto my breast,
Here where thou droop'st lies France. I am very
    feeble —
Of little use it seems to either now.
Well, well — we will go home.
  Bar. In sooth, my Lord,
You do need rest — the burthens of the State
O'ertask your health!
  Rich. [*to* JOSEPH]. I'm patient, see!
  Bar. [*aside*]. His mind
And life are breaking fast!
  Rich. [*overhearing him*]. Irreverent ribald!
If so, beware the falling ruins! Hark!
I tell thee, scorner of these whitening hairs,
When this snow melteth there shall come a flood!
Avaunt! my name is Richelieu — I defy thee!

Walk blindfold on; behind thee stalks the headsman.
Ha! ha! — how pale he is! Heaven save my
country!
[*Falls back in* JOSEPH'S *arms.*

[BARADAS *exit, followed by* DE BERINGHEN, *betraying his exultation by his gestures.*

ACT V.

FOURTH DAY.

SCENE I. — *The Bastile — a Corridor; in the back-ground the door of one of the condemned cells.*

Enter JOSEPH *and* Gaoler.

Gaoler. Stay, father; I will call the Governor.
[*Exit* Gaoler.

Joseph. He has it, then — this Huguet; — so
we learn
From François; — Humph! Now if I can but gain
One moment's access, all is ours! The Cardinal
Trembles 'tween life and death. His life is power;
Smite one — slay both! No Æsculapian drugs,
By learnèd quacks baptized with Latin jargon,
E'er bore the healing which that scrap of parchment
Will medicine to Ambition's flagging heart.
France shall be saved — and Joseph be a bishop.

Enter Governor *and* JOSEPH.

Gov. Father, you wish to see the prisoners Huguet
And the young knight De Mauprat?
Joseph. So my office,
And the Lord Cardinal's order, warrant, son!
Gov. Father, it cannot be: Count Baradas
Has summon'd to the Louvre Sieur de Mauprat.
Joseph. Well, well! But Huguet —
Gov. Dies at noon.
Joseph. At noon!
No moment to delay the pious rites
Which fit the soul for death. Quick — quick — admit me!
Gov. You cannot enter, monk! Such are my orders!
Joseph. Orders, vain man! — the Cardinal still is
minister.
His orders crush all others!
Gov. [*lifting his hat*]. Save his king's!
See, monk, the royal sign and seal affix'd
To the Count's mandate. None may have access
To either prisoner, Huguet or De Mauprat,
Not even a priest, without the special passport
Of Count de Baradas. I'll hear no more!
Joseph. Just Heaven! and are we baffled thus!
Despair!
Think on the Cardinal's power — beware his anger.
Gov. I'll not be menaced, Priest! Besides, the Cardinal
Is dying and disgraced — all Paris knows it.
You hear the prisoner's knell! [*Bell tolls.*

Joseph. I do beseech you —
The Cardinal is *not* dying. But one moment, .
And — hist! — five thousand pistoles! —
Gov. How! a bribe! —
And to a soldier, grey with years of honour!
Begone! —
Joseph. Ten thousand — twenty! —
Gov. Gaoler; put
This monk without our walls.
Joseph. By those grey hairs —
Yea, by this badge [*touching the cross of St. Louis worn by the* Governor] — The guerdon of your valour —
By all your toils — hard days and sleepless nights —
Borne in your country's service, noble son —
Let me but see the prisoner! —
Gov. No!
Joseph. He hath
Secrets of state — papers in which —
Gov. [*interrupting*]. I know —
Such was his message to Count Baradas:
Doubtless the Count will see to it!
Joseph. The Count!
Then not a hope! — You shall —
Gov. Betray my trust!
Never — not one word more. You heard me, gaoler!
Joseph. What can be done? — Distraction! Richelieu yet
Must — what? — I know not! Thought, nerve, strength, forsake me.

Dare you refuse the Church her holiest rights?
  Gov. I refuse nothing — I obey my orders.
  Joseph. And sell your country to her parricides!
Oh, tremble yet! — Richelieu —
  Gov.   Begone!
  Joseph.   Undone! [*Exit* JOSEPH.
  Gov. A most audacious shaveling — interdicted
Above all others by the Count.
  Gaoler.   I hope, sir,
I shall not lose my perquisites. The Sieur
De Mauprat will not be reprieved?
  Gov.   Oh, fear not:
The Count's commands by him who came for Mauprat
Are to prepare headsman and axe by noon;
The Count will give you perquisites enough —
Two deaths in one day!
  Gaoler.   Sir, may Heaven reward him!
Oh, by the way, that troublesome young fellow,
Who calls himself the prisoner Huguet's son
Is here again — implores, weeps, raves to see him.
  Gov. Poor youth, I pity him!

  Enter DE BERINGHEN, *followed by* FRANÇOIS.
  De Ber. [*to* FRANÇOIS]. Now, prithee, friend,
Let go my cloak; you really discompose me.
  Fran. No, they will drive me hence: my father!
      Oh!
Let me but see him once — but once — one moment!
  De Ber. [*to* Governor]. Your servant, Messire; this
      poor rascal, Huguet,

Has sent to see the Count de Baradas
Upon state secrets, that afflict his conscience.
The Count can't leave his Majesty an instant:
I am his proxy.
    Gov.   The Count's word is law!
Again, young scapegrace! How com'st thou admitted?
    De Ber. Oh! a most filial fellow: Huguet's son!
I found him whimpering in the court below.
I pray his leave to say good-bye to father,
Before that very long, unpleasant journey,
Father's about to take. Let him wait here
Till I return.
    Fran.   No; take me with you.
    De Ber.   Nay;
After *me*, friend — the Public first!
    Gov.   The Count's
Commands are strict. No one must visit Huguet
Without his passport.
    De Ber.   Here it is! Pshaw! nonsense!
I'll be your surety. See, my Cerberus,
He is no Hercules!
    Gov.   Well, you're responsible.
Stand there, friend. If, when you come out, my Lord,
The youth slip in, 'tis *your* fault.
    De Ber.   So it is!
    [*Exit through the door of the cell, followed by the* Gaoler.

    Gov. Be calm, my lad. Don't fret so. I had once
A father, too! I'll not be hard upon you,
And so, stand close. I must not *see* you enter:

You understand! Between this innocent youth
And that intriguing monk there is, in truth,
A wide distinction.

    Re-enter Gaoler.

     Come, we'll go our rounds;
I'll give you just one quarter of an hour;
And if my Lord leave first, make my excuse.
Yet stay, the gallery's long and dark: no sentry
Until he reach the grate below. He'd best
Wait till I come. If he should lose the way,
We may not be in call.
  Fran.   I'll tell him, sir.
      [*Exeunt* Governor *and* Gaoler.
He's a wise son that knoweth his own father.
I've forged a precious one! So far, so well!
Alas! what then? this wretch hath sent to Baradas —
Will sell the scroll to ransom life. Oh, Heaven!
On what a thread hangs hope! [*Listens at the door.*
     Loud words — a cry!
     [*Looks through the keyhole.*
They struggle! Ho! — the packet!!!
     [*Tries to open the door.*
     Lost! He has it —
The courtier has it — Huguet, spite his chains,
Grapples! — well done! Now — now! [*Draws back.*
     The gallery's long —
And this is left us!

  [*Drawing his dagger, and standing behind the door. Re-enter* DE BERINGHEN *with the packet.*

Victory!
        Yield it, robber —
Yield it — or die —   [*A short struggle.*
 De Ber.   Oh! ho! — there! —
 Fran. [*grappling with him*]. Death or honour!
         [*Exeunt struggling.*

SCENE II.

The King's *closet at the Louvre. A suite of rooms in perspective at one side.*

BARADAS *and* ORLEANS.

 Bar. All smiles! the Cardinal's swoon of yesterday
Heralds his death to-day. Could he survive,
It would not be as minister — so great
The King's resentment at the priest's defiance!
All smiles! — And yet, should this accursed De Mauprat
Have given our packet to another — 'Sdeath!
I dare not think of it!
 Orle.   You've sent to search him?
 Bar. Sent, sir, to search? — that hireling hands
  may find
Upon him, naked, with its broken seal,
That scroll, whose every word is death! No — No —
These hands alone must clutch that awful secret.
I dare not leave the palace, night nor day,
While Richelieu lives — his minions — creatures —
  spies —
Not one must roach the King!

Orle.   What hast thou done?
Bar. Summon'd De Mauprat hither.
　Orle.   Could this Huguet,
Who pray'd thy presence with so fierce a fervour,
Have thieved the scroll?
　Bar.   Huguet was housed with us,
The very moment we dismiss'd the courier.
It cannot be! a stale trick for reprieve.
But, to make sure, I've sent our trustiest friend
To see and sift him. — Hist! — here comes the King —
How fare you, Sire?

　　　　　　　Enter Louis.
　Louis.   In the same mind. I have
Decided! — Yes, he would forbid your presence,
My brother — yours, my friend, — then Julie, too!
Thwarts — braves — defies — [*suddenly turning to*
　　　Baradas] We make you minister.
Gaston, for you — the bâton of our armies.
You love me, do you not?
　Orle.   Oh, love you, Sire?
[*Aside.*] Never so much as now.
　Bar.   May I deserve
Your trust [*aside*] until you sign your abdication!
My liege, but one way left to daunt De Mauprat,
And Julie to divorce. — We must prepare
The death-writ; what, though sign'd and seal'd? we can
Withhold the enforcement.
　Louis.   Ah, you may prepare it;
We need not urge it to effect.

Bar.   Exactly!
No haste, my liege. [*Looking at his watch and aside.*]
    He may live one hour longer.

                    Enter Courtier.
Cour. The Lady Julie, Sire, implores an audience.
    Louis. Aha! repentant of her folly! — Well,
Admit her.
    Bar.   Sire, she comes for Mauprat's pardon,
And the conditions —
    Louis.   You are minister —
We leave to you our answer.
        [*As* JULIE *enters, the* Captain of the Archers, *by another
            door, and whispers* BARADAS.

    Capt.   The Chevalier
De Mauprat waits below.
    Bar. [*aside*].   Now the despatch!
                        [*Exit with* Officer.

                    Enter JULIE.
    Julie. My liege, you sent for me. I come where Grief
Should come when guiltless, while the name of King
Is holy on the earth! Here, at the feet
Of Power, I kneel for mercy.
    Louis.   Mercy, Julie,
Is an affair of state. The Cardinal should
In this be your interpreter.
    Julie.   Alas!
I know not if that mighty spirit now
Stoop to the things of earth. Nay, while I speak

Perchance he hears the orphan by the throne
Where kings themselves need pardon; O my liege,
Be father to the fatherless; in you
Dwells my last hope!

Enter BARADAS.

Bar. [*aside*]. He has not the despatch;
Smiled, while we search'd, and braves me. — Oh!
Louis [*gently*]. What wouldst thou?
Julie. A single life. — You reign o'er millions. —
What
Is *one man's* life to you? — and yet to *me*
'Tis France — 'tis earth — 'tis everything! — a life —
A human life — my husband's.
Louis [*aside*]. Speak to her,
I am not marble, — give her hope — or —
Bar. Madam,
Vex not your King, whose heart, too soft for justice,
Leaves to his ministers that solemn charge.
[LOUIS *walks up the stage.*
Julie. You *were* his friend.
Bar. I *was* before I loved thee.
Julie. Loved me!
Bar. Hush, Julie: couldst thou misinterpret
My acts, thoughts, motives, nay, my very words,
Here — in this palace?
Julie. Now I know I'm mad;
Even that memory fail'd me.
Bar. I am young,
Well-born and brave as Mauprat! — for thy sake

I peril what he has not — fortune — power;
All to great souls most dazzling. I alone
Can save thee from yon tyrant, now my puppet!
Be mine; annul the mockery of this marriage,
And on the day I clasp thee to my breast
De Mauprat shall be free.
    Julie.   Thou durst not speak
Thus in *his* ear [*pointing to* Louis]. Thou double traitor!
    — tremble!
I will unmask thee.
    Bar.   I will say thou ravest.
And see this scroll! its letters shall be blood!
Go to the King, count with me word for word;
And while you pray the life — I write the sentence!
    Julie. Stay, stay [*rushing to the* King]. You have a
        kind and princely heart,
Tho' sometimes it is silent: you were born
To *power* — it has not flush'd you into madness,
As it doth meaner men. Banish my husband —
Dissolve our marriage — cast me to that grave
Of human ties, where hearts congeal to ice,
In the dark convent's everlasting winter —
(Surely eno' for justice — hate — revenge) —
But spare this life, thus lonely, scath'd, and bloomless;
And when thou stand'st for judgment on thine own,
The deed shall shine beside thee as an angel.
    Louis [*much affected*]. Go, go, to Baradas: annul thy
        marriage,
And —

Julie [*anxiously, and watching his countenance*]. Be his bride!

Louis. A form, a mere decorum; Thou know'st I love thee.

Julie. O thou sea of shame, And not one star!

[*The King goes up the stage, and passes through the suite of rooms at the side, in evident emotion.*

Bar. Well, thy election, Julie; This hand — his grave!

Julie His grave! and I —

Bar. Can save him. — Swear to be mine.

Julie. That were a bitterer death! Avaunt, thou tempter! I did ask his life A boon, and not the barter of dishonour. The heart can break, and scorn you: wreak your malice; Adrien and I will leave you this sad earth, And pass together hand in hand to Heaven!

Bar. You have decided.

[*Withdraws to the side scene for a moment, and returns.*

Listen to me, Lady; I am no base intriguer. I adored thee From the first glance of those inspiring eyes; With thee entwined ambition, hope, the future. *I will not lose thee!* I can place thee nearest — Ay, to the throne — nay, on the throne, perchance; My star is at its zenith. Look upon me; Hast thou decided?

Julie. No, no; you can see
How weak I am: be human, sir — one moment.
  Bar. [*stamping his foot,* DE MAUPRAT *appears at the side of the stage guarded*]. Behold thy husband! — Shall
    he pass to death,
And know thou couldst have saved him?
  Julie. Adrien, speak!
But say you wish to *live!* — if not, your wife,
Your slave, — do with me as you will.
  De Mau. Once more! —
Why this is mercy, Count! Oh, think, my Julie,
Life, at the best, is short, — but love immortal!
  Bar. [*taking* JULIE'S *hand*]. Ah, loveliest —
  Julie. Go, that touch has made me iron.
We have decided — death!
  Bar. [*to* DE MAUPRAT]. Now say to whom
Thou gavest the packet, and thou yet shalt live.
  De Mau. I'll tell thee nothing!
  Bar. Hark, — the rack!
  De Mau. Thy penance
For ever, wretch! — What rack is like the conscience?
  Julie. I shall be with thee soon.
  Bar. [*giving the writ to the* Officer.] Hence, to the
    headsman!

  [*The doors are thrown open. The* Huissier *announces*
    "His Eminence the Cardinal Duke de Richelieu."

  Enter RICHELIEU, *attended by* Gentlemen, Pages, &c.,
    pale, feeble, and leaning on JOSEPH, *followed by three*
    Secretaries of State, *attended by* Sub-Secretaries *with
    papers, &c.*

Julie [*rushing to* RICHELIEU]. You live — you live —
and Adrien shall not die!

Rich. Not if an old man's prayers, himself near death,
Can aught avail' thee, daughter! Count, you now
Hold what I held on earth: — one boon, my Lord,
This soldier's life.

Bar. The stake, — my head! — you said it.
I cannot lose one trick. — Remove your prisoner.

Julie. No! — No! —

Enter LOUIS *from the rooms beyond.*

Rich. [*to* Officer]. Stay, Sir, one moment. My good liege,
Your worn-out servant, willing, Sire, to spare you
Some pain of conscience, would forestall your wishes.
I do resign my office.

De Mau. You!

Julie. All's over!

Rich. My end draws near. These sad ones, Sire, I love them.
I do not ask his life; but suffer justice
To halt, until I can dismiss his soul,
Charged with an old man's blessing.

Louis Surely!

Bar. Sire —

Louis. Silence — small favour to a dying servant.

Rich. You would consign your armies to the bâton
Of your most honoured brother. Sire, so be it!

Your minister, the Count de Baradas;
A most sagacious choice! — Your Secretaries
Of State attend me, Sire, to render up
The ledgers of a realm. I do beseech you,
Suffer these noble gentlemen to learn
The nature of the glorious task that waits them,
Here, in my presence.
  Louis.   You say well, my Lord.
      [*To* Secretaries, *as he seats himself.*
Approach, Sirs.
  Rich.   I — I — faint! — air — air!
   [JOSEPH *and a* Gentleman *assist him to a sofa, placed
    beneath a window.*
         I thank you —
Draw near, my children.
  Bar.   He's too weak to question.
Nay, scarce to speak; all's safe.

SCENE III.

Manent RICHELIEU, MAUPRAT, *and* JULIE, *the last kneeling
beside the* Cardinal; *the* Officer of the Guard *behind* MAUPRAT.
JOSEPH *near* RICHELIEU, *watching the* King. LOUIS. BARADAS
at the back of the King's chair, *anxious and disturbed.* ORLEANS
at a greater distance, careless and triumphant. The Secretaries.
As each Secretary *advances in his turn, he takes the portfolios
from the* Sub-Secretaries.

  First Sec.   The affairs of Portugal,
Most urgent, Sire: One short month since the Duke
Braganza was a rebel.

Louis. And is still!

First Sec. No, Sire, *he has succeeded!* He is now Crown'd King of Portugal — craves instant succour Against the arms of Spain.

Louis. We will not grant it Against his lawful king. Eh, Count?

Bar. No, Sire.

First Sec. But Spain's your deadliest foe: whatever Can weaken Spain must strengthen France. The Cardinal *Would send the succours:* — [*solemnly*] — balance, Sire, of Europe!

Louis. The Cardinal! — balance! — We'll consider. — Eh, Count?

Bar. Yes, Sire; — fall back.

First Sec. But —

Bar. Oh! fall back, Sir.

Joseph. Humph!

Second Sec. The affairs of England, Sire, most urgent: Charles The First has lost a battle that decides One half his realm, — craves moneys, Sire, and succour.

Louis. He shall have both. — Eh, Baradas?

Bar. Yes, Sire. (Oh that despatch! — my veins are fire!)

Rich. [*feebly, but with great distinctness*]. My liege — Forgive me — Charles's cause is lost! A man,

Named Cromwell, risen, — a great man! — your succour
Would fail — your loans be squander'd! — Pause —
reflect.*
Louis. Reflect. — Eh, Baradas?
Bar. Reflect, Sire.
Joseph. Humph!
Louis [*aside*]. I half repent! — No successor to
Richelieu! --
Round me thrones totter! — dynasties dissolve! —
The soil he guards alone escapes the earthquake!
Joseph. Our star not yet eclipsed! — you mark the
King?
Oh! had we the despatch!
Rich. Ah! Joseph! — Child —
Would I could help thee!
Enter Gentleman, *whispers* JOSEPH, *who exit hastily.*
Bar. [*to* Secretary]. Sir, fall back.
Second Sec. But —
Bar. Pshaw, Sir!
Third Sec. [*mysteriously*]. The *secret correspondence*,
Sire, most urgent, —
Accounts of spies — deserters — heretics —
Assassins — poisoners — schemes against yourself! —
Louis. Myself! — most urgent! — [*looking on the
documents.*]
Re-enter JOSEPH *with* FRANÇOIS, *whose pourpoint is
streaked with blood.* FRANÇOIS *passes behind the Car-
dinal's Attendants, and, sheltered by them from the
sight of* BARADAS, &c., *falls at* RICHELIEU'*s feet.*

* See in "Cinq Mars," Vol. V., the striking and brilliant chapter from
which the interlude of the Secretaries is borrowed.

Fran. O! my Lord!
Rich. Thou art bleeding!
Fran. A scratch — I have not fail'd —
[*Gives the packet.*
Rich. Hush! —
[*Looking at the contents.*
Third Sec. [*to* King]. Sire, the Spaniards
Have reinforced their army on the frontiers.
The Duc de Bouillon —
Rich. Hold! — In this department —
A paper — here, Sire, — read yourself — then take
The Count's advice in't.

Enter DE BERINGHEN *hastily, and draws aside* BARADAS.
[RICHELIEU *to* Secretary, *giving an open parchment.*
Bar. [*bursting from* DE BERINGHEN]. What! and reft
it from thee!
Ha! — hold!
Joseph. Fall back, son, it is your turn now!
Bar. Death! — the despatch!
Louis [*reading*]. To Bouillon — and sign'd Orleans! —
Baradas, too! — league with our foes of Spain! —
Lead our Italian armies — what! to Paris! —
Capture the King — my health requires repose —
Make me subscribe my proper abdication —
Orleans, my brother, Regent! — Saints of Heaven!
These are the men I loved!

[BARADAS *draws,* — *attempts to rush out,* — *is arrested.*
— ORLEANS, *endeavouring to escape more quietly,
meets* JOSEPH'S *eye and stops short.* RICHELIEU *falls
back.*

Joseph.   See to the Cardinal!
Bar. He's dying! and I yet shall dupe the King!
Louis [*rushing to* RICHELIEU]. Richelieu! — Lord
      Cardinal! — 'tis *I* resign! —
Reign thou!
  Joseph. Alas! too late! — he faints!
  Louis.   Reign, Richelieu!
  Rich. [*feebly*]. With absolute power? —
  Louis.   Most absolute! — Oh! live!
If not for me — for France!
  Rich.   FRANCE!
  Louis.   Oh! this treason! —
The army — Orleans — Bouillon — Heavens! — the
      Spaniard! —
Where will they be next week? —
  Rich. [*starting up*].   There, — at my feet!
              [*To First and Second Secretary.*
Ere the clock strike! — the Envoys have their answer!
              [*To Third Secretary, with a ring.*
This to De Chavigny — he knows the rest —
No need of parchment here — he must not halt
For sleep — for food. — In *my* name, — MINE! — he will
Arrest the Duc de Bouillon at the head
Of his army! — Ho! there, Count de Baradas,
Thou hast lost the stake! — Away with him!*
      [*As the* Guards *open the folding-doors, a view of the
      ante-room beyond, lined with* Courtiers. BARADAS
      passes through the line.

---

* The passion of the drama requires this catastrophe for Baradas.
He however survived his disgrace, though stripped of all his rapidly-

Ha! — ha! —

[*Snatching* DE MAUPRAT'S *death-warrant from the* Officer.

See here De Mauprat's death-writ, Julie! —
Parchment for battledores! — Embrace your husband! —
At last the old man blesses you!
  Julie.   O joy!
You are saved; you live — I hold you in these arms.
 Mau. Never to part —
 Julie.   No — never, Adrien — never!
 Louis [*peevishly*]. One moment makes a startling cure,
Lord Cardinal.*
 Rich. Ay, Sire, for in one moment there did pass
Into this wither'd frame the might of France! —
My own dear France — I have thee yet — I have
saved thee!
I clasp thee still! — it was thy voice that call'd me
Back from the tomb! — What mistress like our country?
 Louis. For Mauprat's pardon — well! But Julie, —
Richelieu,
Leave me one thing to love! —

---

acquired fortunes; and the daring that belonged to his character won him distinction in foreign service. He returned to France after Richelieu's death, but never regained the same court influence. He had taken the vows of a Knight of Malta, and Louis made him a Prior.

 * The sudden resuscitation of Richelieu (not to strain too much on the real passion which supports him in this scene) is in conformance with the more dissimulating part of his character. The extraordinary mobility of his countenance (latterly so deathlike, save when the mind spoke in the features) always lent itself to stage effect of this nature. The queen-mother said of him, that she had seen him one moment so feeble, cast down, and "semi-mort," that he seemed on the point of giving up the ghost — and the next moment he would start up full of animation, energy, and life.

Rich. A subject's luxury!
Yet, if you must love something, Sire, — *love me!*
 Louis [*smiling in spite of himself*]. Fair proxy for a
  young fresh Demoiselle!
 Rich. Your heart speaks for my clients: — Kneel,
  my children,
And thank your King. —
 Julie. Ah, tears like these, my liege,
Are dews that mount to Heaven.
 Louis. Rise — rise — be happy.
    [RICHELIEU *beckons to* DE BERINGHEN.
 De Ber. [*falteringly*]. My lord — you are — most —
happily — recover'd.
 Rich. But you are pale, dear Beringhen! — this air
Suits not your delicate frame — I long have thought
  so: —
Sleep not another night in Paris: — Go, —
Or else your precious life may be in danger.
Leave France, dear Beringhen!
 De Ber. I shall have time,
More than I ask'd for — to discuss the pâté.
     [*Exit* DE BERINGHEN.
 Rich. [*to* ORLEANS]. For you, repentance — absence —
  and confession! [*To* FRANÇOIS.
Never say *fail* again. — Brave boy! [*To* JOSEPH.
    He'll be —
A Bishop first.
 Joseph. Ah, Cardinal —
 Rich. Ah, Joseph!
  [*To* LOUIS — *as* DE MAUPRAT *and* JULIE *converse apart.*

See, my liege — see thro' plots and counterplots —
Thro' gain and loss — thro' glory and disgrace —
Along the plains, where passionate Discord roars
Eternal Babel — still the holy stream
Of human happiness glides on!
    Louis.   And must we
Thank for *that* also — our prime Minister?
    Rich. No — let us own it: — there is ONE above
Sways the harmonious mystery of the world,
Ev'n better than prime ministers; —
                                    Alas!
Our glories float between the earth and heaven
Like clouds which seem pavilions of the sun,
And are the playthings of the casual wind;
Still, like the cloud which drops on unseen crags
The dews the wild flower feeds on, our ambition
May from its airy height drop gladness down
On unsuspected virtue; — and the flower
May bless the cloud when it hath pass'd away!*

    * The image and the sentiment in the concluding lines are borrowed from a passage in one of the writings attributed to the Cardinal.

MONEY.

> "'Tis a very good world we live in,
> To lend, or to spend, or to give in;
> But to beg, or to borrow, or get a man's own,
> 'Tis the very worst world that ever was known."
>
> — *Old Truism.*

"Und es herrscht der Erde Gott, das Geld." — SCHILLER.

DEDICATED TO

JOHN FORSTER, ESQ.,

AUTHOR OF "THE LIVES OF STATESMEN OF THE COMMONWEALTH."

A SLIGHT MEMORIAL

OF SINCERE RESPECT AND CORDIAL FRIENDSHIP;

ALTHOUGH

(FOR WE ARE ALL HUMAN!)

HE HAS, IN ONE INSTANCE, AND BUT ONE,

SUFFERED HIS JUDGMENT TO BE MISLED BY TOO GREAT A REGARD FOR

"MONEY!"

DRAMATIS PERSONÆ.

LORD GLOSSMORE.
SIR JOHN VESEY, Bart., Knight of the Guelph, F.R.S., F.S.A.
SIR FREDERICK BLOUNT.
STOUT.
GRAVES.
EVELYN.
CAPTAIN DUDLEY SMOOTH.
SHARP.
TOKE.
FRANTZ, *Tailor.*
TABOURET, *Upholsterer.*
MACFINCH, *Jeweller and Silversmith.*
MACSTUCCO, *Architect.*
KITE, *Horse-dealer.*
CRIMSON, *Portrait-painter.*
GRAB, *Publisher.*
PATENT, *Coach-builder.*

Members of the *** *Club, Servants, &c.*

LADY FRANKLIN, *half-sister to Sir John Vesey.*
GEORGINA, *daughter to Sir John.*
CLARA, *companion to Lady Franklin, cousin to Evelyn.*

Scene — LONDON, 1840.

MONEY.

ACT I — SCENE I.

A drawing-room in SIR JOHN VESEY'S *house; folding-doors at the back, which open on another drawing-room. To the right a table, with newspapers, books, &c.; to the left, a sofa writing-table.*

SIR JOHN, GEORGINA.

Sir John [*reading a letter edged with black*]. Yes, he says at two precisely. "Dear Sir John, as since the death of 'my sainted Maria,'" — Hum! — that's his wife; she made him a martyr, and now he makes her a saint!

Geor. Well, as since her death? —

Sir John [*reading*]. "I have been living in chambers, where I cannot so well invite ladies, you will allow me to bring Mr. Sharp, the lawyer, to read the will of the late Mr. Mordaunt (to which I am appointed executor) at your house — your daughter being the nearest relation. I shall be with you at two precisely. — Henry Graves."

Geor. And you really feel sure that poor Mr. Mordaunt has made me his heiress?

Sir John. Ay, the richest heiress in England. Can you doubt it? Are you not his nearest relation? Niece by your poor mother, his own sister. All the time he was making this enormous fortune in India did we ever miss sending him little reminiscences of our disinterested affection? When he was last in England, and you only so high, was not my house his home? Didn't I get a surfeit out of complaisance to his execrable curries and pillaws? Didn't he smoke his hookah — nasty old — that is, poor dear man — in my best drawing-room? And didn't you make a point of calling him your "handsome uncle"? — for the excellent creature was as vain as a peacock, —

Geor. And so ugly! —

Sir John. The dear deceased! Alas, he *was*, indeed; — like a kangaroo in a jaundice! And *if*, after all these marks of attachment, you are *not* his heiress, why then the finest feelings of our nature — the ties of blood — the principles of justice — are implanted in us in vain.

Geor. Beautiful, sir. Was not that in your last speech at the Freemasons' Tavern upon the great Chimney-sweep Question?

Sir John. Clever girl! — what a memory she has! Sit down, Georgy. Upon this most happy — I mean melancholy — occasion, I feel that I may trust you with a secret. You see this fine house — our fine servants — our fine plate — our fine dinners: every one thinks Sir John Vesey a rich man.

Geor. And are you not, papa?

Sir John. Not a bit of it — all humbug, child — all humbug, upon my soul! As you hazard a minnow to hook in a trout, so one guinea thrown out with address is often the best bait for a hundred. There are two rules in life — FIRST, Men are valued not for what they *are*, but what they *seem* to be. SECONDLY, If you have no merit or money of your own, you must trade on the merits and money of other people. My father got the title by services in the army, and died penniless. On the strength of his services I got a pension of £400 a year; on the strength of £400 a year I took credit for £800; on the strength of £800 a year I married your mother with £10,000; on the strength of £10,000 I took credit for £40,000 and paid Dicky Gossip three guineas a week to go about everywhere calling me "Stingy Jack!"

Geor. Ha! ha! A disagreeable nickname.

Sir John. But a valuable reputation. When a man is called stingy, it is as much as calling him rich; and when a man's called rich, why he's a man universally respected. On the strength of my respectability I wheedled a constituency, changed my politics, resigned my seat to a minister, who, to a man of such stake in the country, could offer nothing less in return than a patent office of £.2,000 a year. That's the way to succeed in life. Humbug, my dear! — all humbug, upon my soul.

Geor. I must say that you —

Sir John. Know the world, to be sure. Now, for your fortune, — as I spend more than my income, I can have nothing to leave you; yet, even without counting your uncle, you have always passed for an heiress on the credit of your expectations from the savings of "Stingy Jack." The same with your education. I never grudged anything to make a show — never stuffed your head with histories and homilies; but you draw, you sing, you dance, you walk well into a room; and that's the way young ladies are educated nowadays, in order to become a pride to their parents, and a blessing to their husband — that is, when they have caught him. Apropos of a husband: you know we thought of Sir Frederick Blount.

Geor. Ah, papa, he is charming.

Sir John. He *was so*, my dear, before we knew your poor uncle was dead; but an heiress such as you will be should look out for a duke. — Where the deuce is Evelyn this morning?

Geor. I've not seen him, papa. What a strange character he is! — so sarcastic; and yet he can be agreeable.

Sir John. A humorist — a cynic? one never knows how to take him. My private secretary, — a poor cousin, has not got a shilling, and yet, hang me, if he does not keep us all at a sort of a distance.

Geor. But why do you take him to live with us, papa, since there's no good to be got by it?

Sir John. There you are wrong; he has a great deal of talent: prepares my speeches, writes my pamphlets, looks up my calculations. My Report on the last Commission has got me a great deal of fame, and has put me at the head of the new one. Besides he *is* our cousin — he has no salary: kindness to a poor relation always tells well in the world; and Benevolence is a useful virtue, — particularly when you can have it for nothing! With our other cousin, Clara, it was different: her father thought fit to leave me her guardian, though she had not a penny — a mere useless encumbrance: so, you see, I got my half-sister, Lady Franklin, to take her off my hands.

Geor. How much longer is Lady Franklin's visit to be?

Sir John. I don't know, my dear; the longer the better, — for her husband left her a good deal of money at her own disposal. Ah, here she comes!

SCENE II.

LADY FRANKLIN, CLARA, SIR JOHN, GEORGINA.

Sir John. My dear sister, we were just loud in your praises. But how's this? — not in mourning?

Lady Fran. Why should I go into mourning for a man I never saw?

Sir John. Still, there may be a legacy.

Lady Fran. Then there'll be less cause for affliction! Ha! ha! my dear Sir John, I'm one of those who think feelings a kind of property, and never take credit for them upon false pretences.

Sir John [*aside*]. Very silly woman! But, Clara, I see you are more attentive to the proper decorum: yet you are very, *very*, VERY distantly connected with the deceased — a third cousin, I think?

Clara. Mr. Mordaunt once assisted my father, and these poor robes are all the gratitude I can show him.

Sir John. Gratitude! humph! I am afraid the minx has got expectations.

Lady Frank. So, Mr. Graves is the executor — the will is addressed to him? The same Mr. Graves who is always in black — always lamenting his ill-fortune and his sainted Maria, who led him the life of a dog?

Sir John. The very same. His liveries are black — his carriage is black — he always rides a black galloway — and, faith, if he ever marry again, I think he will show his respect to the sainted Maria by marrying a black woman.

Lady Fran. Ha! ha! we shall see. — [*Aside.*] Poor Graves, I always liked him: he made an excellent husband.

Enter EVELYN [*seats himself, and takes up a book unobserved*].

Sir John. What a crowd of relations this Will brings to light! Mr. Stout, the Political Economist — Lord Glossmore —

Lady Fran. Whose grandfather kept a pawnbroker's shop, and who, accordingly, entertains the profoundest contempt for everything popular, *parvenu,* and plebeian.

Sir John. Sir Frederick Blount —

Lady Fran. Sir Fwedewick Blount, who objects to the letter R as being too wough, and therefore dwops its acquaintance: one of the new class of prudent young gentlemen, who, not having spirits and constitution for the hearty excesses of their predecessors, intrench themselves in the dignity of a lady-like languor. A man of fashion in the last century was riotous and thoughtless — in this he is tranquil and egotistical. He never does anything that is silly, or says anything that is wise. I beg your pardon, my dear; I believe Sir Frederick is an admirer of yours, provided, on reflection, he does not see "what harm it could do him" to fall in love with your beauty and expectations. Then, too, our poor cousin the scholar — Oh, Mr. Evelyn, there you are!

Sir John. Evelyn — the very person I wanted: where have you been all day? Have you seen to those papers? — have you written my epitaph on poor Mordaunt? — Latin, you know? — have you reported my speech at Exeter Hall? — have you looked out the debates on the Customs? — and, oh, have you mended up all the old pens in the study?

Geor. And have you brought me the black floss silk? — have you been to Storr's for my ring? — and, as we cannot go out on this melancholy occasion, did you call at Hookham's for the last HB. and the Comic Annual?

Lady Fran. And did you see what was really the

matter with my bay horse? — did you get me the Opera-box? — did you buy my little Charley his peg-top?

Eve. [*always reading*]. Certainly, Paley is right upon that point; for, put the syllogism thus — [*looking up*] Ma'am — Sir — Miss Vesey — you want something of me? — Paley observes, that to assist even the undeserving tends to the better regulation of our charitable feelings — No apologies — I am quite at your service.

Sir John. Now he's in one of his humours!

Lady Fran. You allow him strange liberties, Sir John.

Eve. You will be the less surprised at that, madam, when I inform you that Sir John allows me nothing else. — I am now about to draw on his benevolence.

Lady Fran. I beg your pardon, sir, and like your spirit. Sir John, I'm in the way, I see; for I know your benevolence is so delicate that you never allow any one to detect it! [*Walks aside.*

Eve. I could not do your commissions to-day — I have been to visit a poor woman, who was my nurse and my mother's last friend. She is very poor, *very* — sick — dying — and she owes six months' rent!

Sir John. You know I should be most happy to do anything for yourself. But the nurse — [*Aside.* Some people's nurses are always ill!] — there are so many impostors about! — We'll talk of it to-morrow. This most mournful occasion takes up all my attention. [*Looking at his watch.*] Bless me! so late! I've letters to write, and — none of the pens are mended! [*Exit.*

Geor. [*taking out her purse*]. I think I will give it to him — and yet, if I don't get the fortune, after all! — Papa allows me so little! — then I *must* have those earrings [*puts up the purse*]. Mr. Evelyn, what is the address of your nurse?

Eve. [*writes and gives it*]. She has a good heart with all her foibles! — Ah! Miss Vesey, if that poor woman had not closed the eyes of my lost mother, Alfred Evelyn would not have been this beggar to your father.

[CLARA *looks over the address.*

Geor. I will certainly attend to it — [*aside*] if I get the fortune.

Sir John [*calling without*]. Georgy, I say!

Geor. Yes, papa. [*Exit.*

[EVELYN *has seated himself again at the table (to the right), and leans his face on his hands.*

Clara. His noble spirit bowed to this! — Ah, at least here I may give him comfort — [*sits down to write*]. But he will recognize my hand.

Lady Frank. What bill are you paying, Clara? — putting up a bank-note?

Clara. Hush! — O Lady Franklin, you are the kindest of human beings. This is for a poor person — I would not have her know whence it came, or she would refuse it. Would you? — he knows *her* hand-writing also!

Lady Frank. Will I — what? give the money myself? with pleasure! Poor Clara — Why this covers all your savings — and I am so rich!

Clara. Nay, I would wish to do all myself! — it is a pride — a duty — it is a joy; and I have so few joys! But, hush! — this way.

[*They retire into the inner room and converse in dumb show.*]

Eve. And thus must I grind out my life for ever! — I am ambitious, and Poverty drags me down; I have learning, and Poverty makes me the drudge of fools! — I love, and Poverty stands like a spectre before the altar! But no, no — if, as I believe, I am but loved again, I will — will — what? — turn opium-eater, and dream of the Eden I may never enter.

Lady Frank. [*to* CLARA]. Yes, I will get my maid to copy and direct this — she writes well, and *her* hand will never be discovered. I will have it done and sent instantly. [*Exit.*

[CLARA *advances to the front of the stage, and seats herself —* EVELYN *reading — Enter* SIR FREDERICK BLOUNT.

SCENE III.

CLARA, EVELYN, SIR FREDERICK BLOUNT.

Blount. No one in the woom! — Oh, Miss Douglas! — Pway don't let me disturb you. Where is Miss Vesey — Georgina?   [*Taking* CLARA'S *chair as she rises.*

Eve. [*looking up, gives* CLARA *a chair and re-seats himself*]. [*Aside.*] Insolent puppy!

Clara. Shall I tell her you are here, Sir Frederick?

Blount. Not for the world. Vewy pwetty girl this companion!

Clara. What did you think of the Panorama the other day, Cousin Evelyn?

Eve. [*reading*]. —

> "I cannot talk with civet in the room,
> A fine puss gentleman that's all perfume!"

Rather good lines these.

Blount. Sir!

Eve. [*offering the book*]. Don't you think so? — Cowper.

Blount [*declining the book*]. Cowper!

Eve. Cowper.

Blount [*shrugging his shoulders, to* CLARA]. Stwange person, Mr. Evelyn! — quite a chawacter! — Indeed the Panowama gives you no idea of Naples — a delightful place. I make it a wule to go there evewy second year — I am vewy fond of twavelling. You'd like Wome (Rome) — bad inns, but vewy fine wuins; gives you quite a taste for that sort of thing!

Eve. [*reading*]. —

"How much a dunce that has been sent to roam
Excels a dunce that has been kept at home!"

Blount [*aside*]. That fellow Cowper says vewy odd things! — Humph! — it is beneath me to quawwell. — [*Aloud.*] It will not take long to wead the will, I suppose. Poor old Mordaunt! — I am his nearest male welation. He was vewy eccentwic. By the way, Miss Douglas, did you wemark my cuwicle? It is bwinging cuwicles into fashion. I should be most happy if you will allow me to dwive you out. Nay — nay — I should, upon my word. [*Trying to take her hand.*

Eve. [*starting up*]. A wasp! — a wasp! — just going to settle. Take care of the wasp, Miss Douglas!

Blount. A wasp! — where! — don't bwing it this way, — some people don't mind them! I've a particular dislike to wasps; they sting damnably!

Eve. I beg pardon — it's only a gadfly.

Enter Servant.

Ser. Sir John will be happy to see you in his study, Sir Frederick. [*Exit Servant.*

Blount. Vewy well. Upon my word, there is something vewy nice about this girl. To be sure, I love

Georgina — but if this one would take a fancy to me [*thoughtfully*] — Well, I don't see what harm it could do me! — *Au plaisir!* [*Exit.*

SCENE IV.

EVELYN and CLARA.

Eve. Clara!

Clara. Cousin!

Eve. And you too are a dependent!

Clara. But on Lady Franklin, who seeks to make me forget it.

Eve. Ay, but can the world forget it? This insolent condescension — this coxcombry of admiration — more galling than the arrogance of contempt! Look you now — Robe Beauty in silk and cashmere — hand Virtue into her chariot — lackey their caprices — wrap them from the winds — fence them round with a golden circle — and Virtue and Beauty are as goddesses both to peasant and to prince. Strip them of the adjuncts — see Beauty and Virtue poor — dependent — solitary — walking the world defenceless! oh, *then* the devotion changes its character — the same crowd gather eagerly around — fools — fops — libertines — not to worship at the shrine, but to sacrifice the victim!

Clara. My cousin, you are cruel!

Eve. Forgive me! There is a something when a man's heart is better than his fortunes, that makes even affection bitter. Mortification for myself — it has ceased to chafe me. I can mock where I once resented. But you — YOU, so delicately framed and nurtured — one slight to you — one careless look — one disdainful tone — makes me feel the true curse of the poor man. His pride gives armour to *his own* breast, but it has no shield to protect another.

Clara. But I, too, have pride of my own — I, too, can smile at the pointless insolence —

Eve. Smile — and he took your hand! Oh, Clara, you know not the tortures that I suffer hourly! When others approach you — young — fair — rich — the sleek darlings of the world — I accuse you of your very beauty — I writhe beneath every smile that you bestow. No — speak not! — my heart has broken its silence, and you shall hear the rest. For you I have endured the weary bondage of this house — the fool's gibe — the hireling's sneer — the bread purchased by toils that should have led me to loftier ends: yes, to see you — hear you — breathe the same air — be ever at hand — that if others slighted, from one at least you might receive the luxury of respect: — for this — for this I have lingered, suffered, and forborne. Oh! Clara, we are orphans both — friendless both: you are all in the world to me: turn not away — my very soul speaks in those words — I LOVE YOU!

Clara. No — Evelyn — Alfred — No! say it not; think it not! it were madness.

Eve. Madness! — nay, hear me yet. I am poor,

penniless — a beggar for bread to a dying servant. True! — But I have a heart of iron! I have knowledge — patience — health, — and my love for you gives me at last ambition! I have trifled with my own energies till now, for I despised all things till I loved you. With you to toil for — your step to support — your path to smooth — and I — I poor Alfred Evelyn — promise at last to win for you even fame and fortune! Do not withdraw your hand — *this* hand — shall it not be mine?

Clara. Ah, Evelyn! Never — never!

Eve. Never.

Clara. Forget this folly; our union is impossible, and to talk of love were to deceive both!

Eve. [*bitterly*]. Because I am poor!

Clara. And *I too!* A marriage of privation — of penury — of days that dread the morrow! I have seen such a lot! Never return to this again.

Eve. Enough — you are obeyed. I deceived myself — ha! — ha! — I fancied that I too was loved. I, whose youth is already half gone with care and toil! — whose mind is soured — whom nobody *can* love — who ought to have loved no one!

Clara [*aside*]. And if it were only *I* to suffer, or perhaps to starve? — Oh, what shall I say? [*Aloud.*] Evelyn — Cousin?

Eve. Madam.

Clara. Alfred — I — I —
Eve. Reject me!
Clara. Yes! It is past! [*Exit.*

Eve. Let me think. It was yesterday her hand trembled when mine touched it. And the rose I gave her — yes, she pressed her lips to it once when she seemed as if she saw me not. But it was a trap — a trick — for I was as poor then as now. This will be a jest for them all! Well, courage! it is but a poor heart that a coquet's contempt can break! And now, that I care for no one, the world is but a great chessboard, and I will sit down in earnest and play with Fortune!

Enter LORD GLOSSMORE, *preceded by* Servant.

Ser. I will tell Sir John, my Lord!
[EVELYN *takes up the newspaper.*

Gloss. The secretary — hum! Fine day, sir; any news from the East?

Eve. Yes! — all the wise men have gone back there!

Gloss. Ha, ha! — not all, for here comes Mr. Stout, the great political economist.

SCENE V.

STOUT, GLOSSMORE, EVELYN.

Stout. Good morning, Glossmore.

Gloss. Glossmore! — the parvenu!

Stout. Afraid I might be late — been detained at the Vestry — Astonishing how ignorant the English poor are! Took me an hour and a half to beat it into the head of a stupid old widow, with nine children, that to allow her three shillings a week was against all the rules of public morality!

Eve. Excellent! — admirable! — your hand, sir!

Gloss. What! you approve such doctrines, Mr. Evelyn? Are old women only fit to be starved?

Eve. Starved! popular delusion! Observe, my Lord — to squander money upon those who starve is only to afford encouragement to starvation!

Stout. A very superior person that!

Gloss. Atrocious principles! Give me the good old times, when it was the duty of the rich to succour the distressed.

Eve. On second thoughts, *you* are right, my Lord. I, too, know a poor woman — ill — dying — in want. Shall *she*, too, perish?

Gloss. Perish! horrible! — in a Christian country! Perish! Heaven forbid!

Eve. [*holding out his hand*]. What, then, will you give her?

Gloss. Ehem! Sir — the parish ought to give.

Stout. No! — no! — no! Certainly not! [*with great vehemence*].

Gloss. No! no! But I say, yes! yes! And if the parish refuse to maintain the poor, the only way left to a man of firmness and resolution, holding the principles that I do, and adhering to the constitution of our fathers, is to force the poor *on* the parish by never giving them a farthing one's self.

SCENE VI.

Sir John, Blount, Lady Franklin, Georgina, Glossmore, Stout, Evelyn.

Sir John. How d'ye do? — Ah! How d'ye do, gentlemen? This is a most melancholy meeting! The poor deceased! what a man he was!

Blount. I was chwistened Fwedewick after him! He was my first cousin.

Sir John. And Georgina his own niece — next of kin! — an excellent man, though odd — a kind heart, but no liver! I sent him twice a year thirty dozen of the Cheltenham waters. It's a comfort to reflect on these little attentions at such a time.

Stout. And I, too, sent him the Parliamentary debates regularly, bound in calf. He was my second cousin — sensible man — and a follower of Malthus: never married to increase the surplus population, and fritter away his money on his own children. And now —

Eve. He reaps the benefit of celibacy in the prospective gratitude of every cousin he had in the world!

Lady Frank. Ha! ha! ha!

Sir John. Hush! hush! decency, Lady Franklin; decency!

Enter Servant.

Ser. Mr. Graves — Mr. Sharp.

Sir John. Oh, here's Mr. Graves; that's Sharp the lawyer, who brought the will from Calcutta.

SCENE VII.

GRAVES, SHARP, SIR JOHN, &c.

Chorus of SIR JOHN, GLOSSMORE, BLOUNT, STOUT.

Ah, sir — Ah, Mr. Graves!

[GEORGINA *holds her handkerchief to her eyes.*

Sir John. A sad occasion!

Graves. But everything in life is sad. Be comforted, Miss Vesey. True, you have lost an uncle; but I — I have lost a wife — such a wife! — the first of her sex — and the second cousin of the defunct! Excuse me, Sir John; at the sight of your mourning my wounds bleed afresh.

[Servants *hand round wine and sandwiches.*

Sir John. Take some refreshment — a glass of wine.

Graves. Thank you! — (very fine sherry!) — Ah! my poor sainted Maria! Sherry was *her* wine: everything reminds me of Maria! Ah, Lady Franklin! you knew her. Nothing in life can charm me now. — [*Aside.*] A monstrous fine woman that!

Sir John. And now to business. Evelyn, you may retire.

Sharp [*looking at his notes*]. Evelyn — any relation to Alfred Evelyn?

Eve. The same.

Sharp. Cousin to the deceased, seven times removed. Be seated, sir; there may be some legacy, though trifling: all the relations, however distant, should be present.

Lady Fran. Then Clara is related — I will go for her. [*Exit.*

Geor. Ah, Mr. Evelyn; I hope you will come in for something — a few hundreds, or even more.

Sir John. Silence! Hush! Wugh! ugh! Attention!

[*While the Lawyer opens the will, re-enter* LADY FRANKLIN *and* CLARA.

Sharp. The will is very short — being all personal property. He was a man that always came to the point.

Sir John. I wish there were more like him! — [*Groans and shakes his head.*

[*Chorus groan and shake their heads.*

Sharp [*reading*]. "I, Frederick James Mordaunt, of Calcutta, being at the present date of sound mind, though infirm body, do hereby give, will and bequeath — Inprimis, To my second cousin, Benjamin Stout, Esq., of Pall Mall, London —

[*Chorus exhibit lively emotion.*

Being the value of the Parliamentary Debates with which he has been pleased to trouble me for some time past — deducting the carriage thereof, which he always forgot to pay — the sum of £ 14. 2 *s.* 4 *d.*

[*Chorus breathe more freely.*

Stout. Eh, what? — £ 14? Oh, hang the old miser!

Sir John. Decency — decency! Proceed, sir.

Sharp. "Item. — To Sir Frederick Blount, Baronet, my nearest male relative —"

[*Chorus exhibit lively emotion.*

Blount. Poor old boy!

[GEORGINA *puts her arm over* BLOUNT'S *chair.*

Sharp. "Being, as I am informed, the best-dressed young gentleman in London, and in testimony to the only merit I ever heard he possessed, the sum of £ 500 to buy a dressing-case."

[*Chorus breathe more freely;* GEORGINA *catches her father's eye, and removes her arm.*

Blount [*laughing confusedly*]. Ha! ha! ha! Vewy poor wit — low! — vewy — vewy low!

Sir John. Silence, now, will you?

Sharp. "Item. — To Charles Lord Glossmore — who asserts that he is my relation — my collection of dried butterflies, and the pedigree of the Mordaunts from the reign of King John."
[*Chorus as before.*
Gloss. Butterflies! — Pedigree! — I disown the plebeian!
Sir John [*angrily*]. Upon my word, this is too revolting! Decency! Go on.
Sharp. "Item. — To Sir John Vesey, Baronet, Knight of the Guelph, F.R.S., F.S.A., &c."
[*Chorus as before.*
Sir John. Hush! Now it is really interesting!
Sharp. "Who married my sister, and who sends me every year the Cheltenham waters, which nearly gave me my death, I bequeath — the empty bottles."
Sir John. Why, the ungrateful, rascally, old —
Chorus. Decency, Sir John — decency.
Sharp. "Item. — To Henry Graves, Esq., of the Albany —" [*Chorus as before.*
Graves. Pooh! gentlemen — my usual luck — not even a ring, I dare swear!
Sharp. "The sum of £5,000 in the Three per Cents."
Lady Fran. I wish you joy!
Graves. Joy — pooh! Three per Cents! — Funds sure to go! Had it been *land*, now — though only an acre! — just like my luck.

Sharp. "Item, — To my niece Georgina Vesey —"
[*Chorus as before.*
Sir John. Ah, now it comes!
Sharp. "The sum of £ 10,000 India Stock, being, with her father's reputed savings, as much as a single woman ought to possess."
Sir John. And what the devil, then, does the old fool do with all his money?
Chorus. Really, Sir John, this is too revolting. Decency! Hush!
Sharp. "And with the aforesaid legacies and exceptions, I do will and bequeath the whole of my fortune, in India Stock, Bonds, Exchequer Bills, Three per Cent. Consols, and in the Bank of Calcutta, (constituting him hereby sole residuary legatee and joint executor with the aforesaid Henry Graves, Esq.) to Alfred Evelyn, now, or formerly of Trinity College, Cambridge —
[*Universal excitement.*
Being I am told, an oddity, like myself — the only one of my relations who never fawned on me; and, who having known privation, may the better employ wealth." — And now, Sir, I have only to wish you joy, and give you this letter from the deceased — I believe it is important.
Eve. [*crossing over to* CLARA]. Ah, Clara, if you had but loved me!
Clara [*turning away*]. And his wealth, even more than poverty, separates us for ever!
[*Omnes crowd round to congratulate* EVELYN.

Sir John [*to* GEORGINA]. Go, child — put a good face on it — he's an immense match! My dear fellow, I wish you joy: you are a great man now — a very great man!

Eve. [*aside*]. And *her* voice alone is silent!

Lord Gloss. If I can be of any use to you —

Stout. Or I, sir —

Blount. Or I! Shall I put you up at the clubs?

Sharp. You will want a man of business. I transacted all Mr. Mordaunt's affairs.

Sir John. Tush, tush! Mr. Evelyn is at home *here* — always looked on him as a son! Nothing in the world we would not do for him! Nothing!

Eve. Lend me £ 10 for my old nurse!

[*Chorus put their hands into their pockets.*

ACT II. — SCENE I.

An anteroom in EVELYN'S *new house; at one corner, behind a large screen,* MR. SHARP *writing at a desk, books and parchments before him. —* MR. CRIMSON, *the portrait-painter;* MR. GRAB, *the publisher;* MR. MACSTUCCO, *the architect;* MR. TABOURET, *the upholsterer;* MR. MACFINCH, *the silversmith;* MR. PATENT, *the coachmaker;* MR. KITE, *the horse-dealer;* MR. FRANTZ, *the tailor.* — (*Servants cross to and fro the stage.*)

Patent [*to* FRANTZ, *showing a drawing*]. Yes, sir; this is the Evelyn vis-à-vis! No one more the fashion than Mr. Evelyn. Money makes the man, sir.

Frantz. But de tailor, de schneider, make de gentleman! It is Mr. Frantz, of St. James's, who take his measure and his cloth, and who make de fine handsome noblemen and gentry, where de faders and de mutters make only de ugly little naked boys!

Macstuc. He's a mon o' teeste, Mr. Evelyn. He taulks o' buying a veela (villa), just to pool down and build oop again. — Ah, Mr. Macfinch! a design for a piece of pleete, eh?

Macfinch [*showing the drawing*]. Yees, sir; the shield o' Alexander the Great, to hold ices and lemonade! It will coost two thousand poon'!

Macstuc. And it's dirt cheap — ye're Scotch, arn't ye?

Macfinch. Aberdounshire! — scraitch me, and I'll scraitch you!

[*Door at the back thrown open. — Enter* EVELYN.

Eve. A levee, as usual. Good day. Ah, Tabouret, your designs for the draperies; very well. And what do you want, Mr. Crimson?

Crim. Sir, if you'd let me take your portrait, it would make my fortune. Every one says you're the finest judge of paintings.

Eve. Of paintings! paintings! Are you sure I'm a judge of paintings?

Crim. Oh, sir, didn't you buy the great Correggio for 4,000.

Eve. True — I see. So £ 4,000 makes me an excellent judge of paintings. I'll call on you, Mr. Crimson, — good day. Mr. Grab—oh, you're the publisher who once refused me £ 5 for a poem? You are right, it was a sad doggerel.

Grab. Doggerel! Mr. Evelyn, it was sublime! But times were bad then.

Eve. Very bad times with me.

Grab. But now, sir, if you will give me the preference, I'll push it, sir, — I'll push it! I only publish for poets in high life, sir; and a gentleman of your station ought to be pushed! — £ 500 for the poem, sir!

Eve. £500 when I don't want it, where £5 once would have seemed a fortune.

"Now I am rich, what value in the lines!
How the wit brightens — how the sense refines!"

[*Turns to the rest who surround him.*

Kite. Thirty young horses from Yorkshire, sir!

Patent [*showing drawing*]. The Evelyn vis-à-vis!

Macfinch [*showing drawing*]. The Evelyn salver!

Frantz [*opening his bundle, and with dignity*]. Sare, I have brought de coat — de great Evelyn coat.

Eve. Oh, go to —— that is, go home! Make me as celebrated for vis-à-vis, salvers, furniture, and coats, as I already am for painting, and shortly shall be for poetry. I resign myself to you — go!

[*Exeunt* MACFINCH, PATENT, &c.

Enter STOUT.

Eve. Stout, you look heated!

Stout. I hear you have just bought the great Groginhole property.

Eve. It is true. Sharp says it's a bargain.

Stout. Well, my dear friend Hopkins, member for Groginhole, can't live another month — but the interests of mankind forbid regret for individuals! The patriot Popkins intends to start for the borough the instant Hopkins is dead! — your interest will secure his election! — now is your time! put yourself forward in the march of enlightenment! — By all that is bigoted, here comes Glossmore!

SCENE II.

STOUT, GLOSSMORE, EVELYN; SHARP *still at his desk.*

Gloss. So lucky to find you at home! Hopkins, of Groginhole, is not long for this world. Popkins, the brewer, is already canvassing underhand (so very ungentlemanlike!). Keep your interest for young Lord Cipher — a most valuable candidate. This is an awful moment — the CONSTITUTION depends on his return! Vote for Cipher.

Stout. Popkins is your man!

Eve. [*musingly*]. Cipher and Popkins — Popkins and Cipher! Enlightenment and Popkins — Cipher and the Constitution! I AM puzzled! Stout, I am not known at Groginhole.

Stout. Your *property's* known there!

Eve. But purity of election — independence of votes ——

Stout. To be sure: Cipher bribes *abominably*. Frustrate his schemes — preserve the liberties of the borough — turn every man out of his house who votes against enlightenment and Popkins!

Eve. Right! — down with those who take the liberty to admire any liberty except *our* liberty! That *is* liberty!

Gloss. Cipher has a stake in the country — will have £50,000 a year — Cipher will never give a vote without considering beforehand how people of £50,000 a year will be affected by the motion.

Eve. Right; for as without law there would be no property, so to be the law for property is the only proper property of law! — That *is* law!

Stout. Popkins is all for economy — there's a sad waste of the public money — they give the Speaker £5,000 a year, when I've a brother-in-law who takes the chair at the vestry, and who assures me confidentially he'd consent to be speaker for half the money?

Gloss. Enough, Mr. Stout — Mr. Evelyn has too much at stake for a leveller.

Stout. And too much sense for a bigot.

Eve. Mr. Evelyn has no politics at all! — Did you ever play at *battledore?*

Both. Battledore?

Eve. Battledore! — that is a contest between two parties: both parties knock about something with singular skill — something is kept up — high — low — here — there — everywhere — nowhere! How grave are the players! how anxious the bystanders! how noisy the battledores! But when this something falls to the ground, only fancy — it's nothing but cork and feather! Go, and play by yourselves — I'm no hand at it!

Stout [*aside*]. Sad ignorance! — Aristocrat!

Gloss. Heartless principles! — Parvenu!

Stout. Then you don't go *against* us? — I'll bring Popkins to-morrow.

Gloss. Keep yourself free till I present Cipher to you.

Stout. I must go to inquire after Hopkins. The return of Popkins will be an era in history.
[*Exit.*

Gloss. I must be off to the club — the eyes of the country are upon Groginhole. If Cipher fail, the constitution is gone! [*Exit.*

Eve. Both sides alike! Money *versus* Man! — Sharp, come here — let me look at you! You are my agent, my lawyer, my man of business. I believe you honest; — but what *is* honesty? — where does it exist? — in what part of us?

Sharp. In the heart, I suppose, sir.

Eve. Mr. Sharp, it exists in the breeches-pocket! Observe: I lay this piece of yellow earth on the table — I contemplate you both; the man there — the gold here! Now, there is many a man in those streets honest as you are, who moves, thinks, feels and reasons as well as we do; excellent in form — imperishable in soul; who if his pockets were three days empty, would sell thought, reason, body, and soul too, for that little coin! Is that the fault of the man? — no! it is the fault of mankind! God made man; behold what mankind have made a god! When *I* was poor, I hated the world; now I am rich, I despise it! Fools — knaves — hypocrites! — By the bye, Sharp, send £100 to the poor bricklayer whose house was burned down yesterday —

Enter GRAVES.

Ah, Graves, my dear friend! what a world this is! — a cur of a world, that fawns on its master, and bites the beggar! Ha! ha! it fawns on *me* now, for the beggar has bought the cur.

Graves. It is an atrocious world! — But astronomers say that there is a travelling comet which must set it on fire one day, — and that's some comfort!

Eve. Every hour brings its gloomy lesson — the temper sours — the affections wither — the heart hardens into stone! Zounds, Sharp! what do you stand gaping there for? — have you no bowels? — why don't you go and see to the bricklayer? [*Exit* SHARP.

SCENE III.

GRAVES *and* EVELYN.

Eve. Graves, of all my new friends — and their name is Legion — you are the only one I esteem; there is sympathy between us — we take the same views of life. I am cordially glad to see you!

Graves [*groaning*]. Ah! why should you be glad to see a man so miserable?

Eve. Because I am miserable myself.

Graves. You! Pshaw! you have not been condemned to lose a wife!

Eve. But, plague on it, man, I may be condemned to take one! — Sit down, and listen. I want a confidant! — Left fatherless, when yet a boy, my poor mother grudged herself food to give me education. Some one had told her that learning was better than house and land — that's a lie, Graves.

Graves. A scandalous lie, Evelyn!

Eve. On the strength of that lie I was put to school — sent to college, a sizar. Do you know what a sizar is? In pride he is a gentleman — in knowledge he is a scholar — and he crawls about, amidst gentlemen and scholars, with the livery of a pauper on his back! I carried off the great prizes — I became distinguished — I looked to a high degree, leading to a fellowship; that is, an independence for myself — a home for my mother. One day a young lord insulted me — I retorted — he struck me — refused apology — refused redress. I was a sizar! — a Pariah! — a thing to *be* struck! Sir, I was at least a man, and I horsewhipped him in the hall before the eyes of the whole College! A few days, and the lord's chastisement was forgotten. The next day the sizar was expelled — the career of a life blasted! That is the difference between Rich and Poor: it takes a whirlwind to move the one — a breath may uproot the other! I came to London. As long as my mother lived, I had one to toil for; and I did toil — did hope — did struggle to be something yet. She died, and then, somehow, my spirit broke — I resigned myself to my fate; the Alps above me seemed too high to ascend — I ceased to care what became of me. At last I submitted to be the poor relation — the hanger-on and gentleman-lackey of Sir John Vesey.

But I had an object in that — there was one in that house whom I had loved at the first sight.

Graves. And were you loved again?

Eve. I fancied it, and was deceived. Not an hour before I inherited this mighty wealth I confessed my love and was rejected because I was poor. Now, mark: you remember the letter which Sharp gave me when the will was read?

Graves. Perfectly; what were the contents?

Eve. After hints, cautions, and admonitions — half in irony, half in earnest (Ah, poor Mordaunt had known the world!), it proceeded — but I'll read it to you: — "Having selected you as my heir, because I think money a trust to be placed where it seems likely to be best employed, I now — not impose a condition, but ask a favour. If you have formed no other and insuperable attachment, I could wish to suggest your choice: my two nearest female relations are my niece Georgina, and my third cousin, Clara Douglas, the daughter of a once dear friend. If you could see in either of these one whom you could make your wife, such would be a marriage that, if I live long enough to return to England, I would seek to bring about before I die." My friend, this is not a legal condition — the fortune does not *rest* on it! yet, need I say that my gratitude considers it a moral obligation? Several months have elapsed since thus called upon — I ought now to decide: you hear the names — Clara Douglas is the woman who rejected me!

Graves. But now she would accept you!

Eve. And do you think I am so base a slave to passion, that I would owe to my gold what was denied to my affection?

Graves. But you must choose one, in common gratitude; you *ought* to do so — yes, there you are right. Besides, you are constantly at the house — the world observes it: you must have raised hopes in one of the girls. Yes; it is time to decide between her whom you love and her whom you do not!

Eve. Of the two, then, I would rather marry where I should exact the least. A marriage, to which each can bring sober esteem and calm regard, may not be happiness, but it may be content. But to marry one whom you could adore, and whose heart is closed to you — to yearn for the treasure, and only to claim the casket — to worship the statue that you never may warm to life — Oh! such a marriage would be a hell, the more terrible because Paradise was in sight.

Graves. Georgina is pretty, but vain and frivolous. — [*Aside.*] But he has no right to be fastidious — he has never known Maria! — [*Aloud.*] Yes, my dear friend, now I think on it, you *will* be as wretched as myself! When you are married, we will mingle our groans together!

Eve. You may misjudge Georgina; she may have a nobler nature than appears on the surface. On the day, but before the hour, in which the will was read, a letter, in a strange or disguised hand, signed "*From *an unknown friend to Alfred Evelyn,*" and enclosing what to a girl would have been a considerable sum, was sent to a poor woman for whom I had implored charity, and whose address I had only given to Georgina.

Graves. Why not assure yourself?

Eve. Because I have not dared. For sometimes, against my reason, I have hoped that it might be Clara! [*taking a letter from his bosom and looking at it*]. No, I can't recognize the hand. Graves, I detest that girl.

Graves. Who? Georgina?

Eve. No; Clara! But I've already, thank Heaven! taken some revenge upon her. Come nearer. — [*Whispers.*] I've bribed Sharp to say that Mordaunt's letter to me contained a codicil leaving Clara Douglas £20,000.

Graves. And didn't it? How odd, then, not to have mentioned her in his will!

Eve. One of his caprices: besides, Sir John wrote him word that Lady Franklin had adopted her. But I'm glad of it — I've paid the money — she's no more a dependent. No one can insult her now — she owes it all to me, and does not guess it, man — does not guess it! — owes it to me, — me, whom she rejected; — me, the poor scholar! — Ha! ha! — there's some spite in that, eh?

Graves. You're a fine fellow, Evelyn, and we understand each other. Perhaps Clara may have seen the address, and dictated this letter, after all!

Eve. Do you think so? — I'll go to the house this instant!

Graves. Eh? Humph! Then I'll go with you. That Lady Franklin is a fine woman! If she were not so gay, I think — I could —

Eve. No, no; don't think any such thing; women are even worse than men.

Graves. True; to love is a boy's madness!

Eve. To feel is to suffer.

Graves. To hope is to be deceived.

Eve. I have done with romance!

Graves. Mine is buried with Maria!

Eve. If Clara did but write this —

Graves. Make haste, or Lady Franklin will be out! — A vale of tears! — a vale of tears!

Eve. A vale of tears, indeed! [*Exeunt.*

Re-enter GRAVES *for his hat.*

Graves. And I left my hat behind me! Just like my luck! If I had been bred a hatter, little boys would have come into the world without heads.* [*Exit.*

---

* For this melancholy jest Mr. Graves is indebted to a poor Italian poet.

SCENE IV.

Drawing-rooms at Sir John Vesey's, *as in Act I., Scene I.*

LADY FRANKLIN, CLARA, Servant.

Lady Frank. Past two, and I have so many places to go to! Tell Philipps I want the carriage directly — instantly.

Ser. I beg pardon, my Lady; Philipps told me to say the young horse had fallen lame, and could not be used to-day.　　　　　　　　　　　　　　　　[*Exit.*

Lady Frank. Well, on second thoughts, that is lucky; now I have an excuse for not making a great many tedious visits. I must borrow Sir John's horses for the ball to-night. Oh, Clara, you must see my new turban from Carson's — the prettiest thing in the world, and so becoming!

Clara. Ah, Lady Franklin, you'll be so sorry — but — but —

Lady Frank. But what?

Clara. Such a misfortune! poor Smith is in tears — I promised to break it to you. Your little Charley had been writing his copy, and spilt the ink on the table; and Smith not seeing it — and taking out the turban to put in the pearls as you desired — she — she —

Lady Frank. Ha! ha! laid it on the table, and the ink spoilt it. Ha! ha! — how well I can fancy the face she made! Seriously, on the whole it is fortunate; for I think I look best, after all, in the black hat and feathers.

Clara. Dear Lady Franklin, you really have the sweetest temper!

Lady Frank. I hope so — for it's the most becoming turban a woman can wear! Think of that when you marry. Oh, talking of marriage, I've certainly made a conquest of Mr. Graves.

Clara. Mr. Graves! I thought he was inconsolable.

Lady Frank. For his sainted Maria! Poor man! not contented with plaguing him while she lived, she must needs haunt him now she is dead.

Clara. But why does he regret her?

Lady Frank. Why? Because he has everything to make him happy — easy fortune, good health, respectable character. And since it is his delight to be miserable, he takes the only excuse the world will allow him. For the rest — it's the way with widowers; that is, whenever they mean to marry again. But, my dear Clara, you seem absent — pale — unhappy — tears, too?

Clara. No — no — not tears. No!

Lady Frank. Ever since Mr. Mordaunt left you £20,000 every one admires you. Sir Frederick is desperately smitten.

Clara [*with disdain.*] Sir Frederick!

Lady Frank. Ah! Clara, be comforted — I know your secret: I am certain that Evelyn loves you.

Clara. He did — it is past now. He misconceived me when he was poor; and now he is rich, it is not for me to explain.

Lady Frank. My dear child, happiness is too rare to be sacrificed to a scruple. Why does he come here so often?

Clara. Perhaps for Georgina!

Enter SIR JOHN, *and turns over the books, &c., on the table, as if to look for the newspaper.*

Lady Frank. Pooh! Georgina is my niece; she is handsome and accomplished — but her father's worldliness has spoilt her nature — she is not worthy of Evelyn! Behind the humour of his irony there is something noble — something that may yet be great. For his sake as well as yours, let me at least —

Clara. Recommend me to his pity? Ah, Lady Franklin! if he addressed me from dictation, I should again refuse him. No; if he cannot read my heart — if he will not seek to read it, let it break unknown.

Lady Frank. You mistake me, my dear child: let me only tell him that you dictated that letter — that you sent that money to his old nurse. Poor Clara! it was your little all. He will then know, at least, if avarice be your sin.

Clara. He would have guessed it had *his* love have been like *mine.*

Lady Frank. Guessed it! — nonsense! The handwriting unknown to him — every reason to think it came from Georgina.

Sir John [*aside*]. Hum! Came from Georgina!

Lady Frank. Come, *let* me tell him *this.* I know the effect it would have upon his choice.

Clara. Choice! oh, that humiliating word! No, Lady Franklin, no! Promise me!

Lady Frank. But —

Clara. No! Promise — faithfully — sacredly.

Lady Frank. Well, I promise.

Clara. You know how fearful is my character — no infant is more timid: if a poor spider cross the floor, you often laugh to see me grow pale and tremble; and yet I would lay this hand upon the block — I would walk barefoot over the ploughshare of the old ordeal — to save Alfred Evelyn one moment's pain. But I have refused to share his poverty, and I should die with shame if he thought I had now grown enamoured of his wealth. My kind friend, you will keep your promise?

Lady Frank. Yes, since it must be so.

Clara. Thanks. I — I — forgive me — I am not well. [*Exit.*

Lady Frank. What fools these girls are! — they take as much pains to lose a husband as a poor widow does to get one!

Sir John. Have you seen "The Times" newspaper? Where the deuce is the newspaper? I can't find "The Times" newspaper.

Lady Frank. I think it is in my room. Shall I fetch it?

Sir John. My dear sister — you're the best creature. Do! [*Exit* LADY FRANKLIN.

Ugh! you unnatural conspirator against your own family! What can this *letter* be? Ah! I recollect something.

Enter GEORGINA.

Geor. Papa, I want —

Sir John. Yes, I know what you want well enough! Tell me — were you aware that Clara had sent money to that old nurse Evelyn bored us about the day of the will?

Geor. No! He gave me the address, and I promised, if —

Sir John. Gave you *the address?* — that's lucky! Hush!

Enter Servant.

Mr. Graves — Mr. Evelyn.

SCENE V.

GRAVES, EVELYN, SIR JOHN, GEORGINA, LADY FRANKLIN.

Lady Frank. [*returning*]. Here is the newspaper.

Graves. Ay — read the newspaper! — they'll tell you what this world is made of. Daily calendars of roguery and woe! Here, advertisements from quacks, money-lenders, cheap warehouses, and spotted boys with two heads. So much for dupes and impostors! Turn to the other column — police reports, bankruptcies, swindling, forgery, and a biographical sketch of the snub-nosed man who murdered his own three little cherubs at Pentonville. Do you fancy these but exceptions to the *general* virtue and health of the nation? — Turn to the leading articles; and your hair will stand on end at the horrible wickedness or melancholy idiotism of that half the population who think differently from yourself. In my day I have seen already eighteen crises, six annihilations of Agriculture and Commerce, four overthrows of the Church, and three last, final, awful, and irremediable destructions of the entire Constitution. And that's a newspaper!

Lady Frank. Ha! ha! your usual vein! always so amusing and good-humoured!

Graves [*frowning and very angry*]. Ma'am — good-humoured! —

Lady Frank. Ah! you should always wear that agreeable smile; you look so much younger — so much handsomer — when you smile!

Graves [*softened*]. Ma'am — A charming creature, upon my word!

Lady Frank. You have not seen the last HB.? It is excellent. I think it might make you *laugh.* But, by the bye, I don't think you can laugh.

Graves. Ma'am — I have not laughed since the death of my sainted Ma —

Lady Frank. Ah! and that spiteful Sir Frederick says you never laugh, because — But you'll be angry?

Graves. Angry! — pooh! I despise Sir Frederick too much to let anything he says have the smallest influence over me! He says I don't laugh, because —

Lady Frank. You have lost your front teeth!

Graves. Lost my front teeth! Upon my word! Ha! ha! ha! That's too good — capital! Ha! ha! ha! [*laughing from ear to ear*].

Lady Frank. Ha! ha! ha!

[*They retire to the table in the inner drawing-room.*

Eve. [*aside*]. Of course Clara will not appear! — avoids me as usual! But what do I care? — what is she to me? Nothing! I'll swear this is her glove! — no one else has so small a hand. She'll miss it — so — so —! Nobody's looking — I'll keep it, just to vex her.

Sir John [*to* GEORGINA]. Yes — yes — leave me to manage: you took his portrait, as I told you?

Geor. Yes — but I could not catch the expression. I got Clara to touch it up.

Sir John. That girl's always in the way!

Enter CAPTAIN DUDLEY SMOOTH.

Smooth. Good morning, dear John. Ah, Miss Vesey, you have no idea of the conquests you made at Almack's last night!

Eve. [*examining him curiously while* SMOOTH *is talking to* GEORGINA.] And that's the celebrated Dudley Smooth!

Sir John. More commonly called Deadly Smooth! — the finest player at whist, écarté, billiards, chess, and picquet, between this and the Pyramids — the sweetest manners! — always calls you by your Christian name. But take care how you play at cards with him!

Eve. He does not cheat, I suppose?

Sir John. Hist! *No!* — but he always *wins!* Eats up a brace of lords and a score or two of guardsmen every season, and runs through a man's fortune like a course of the Carlsbad waters. He's an uncommonly clever fellow!

Eve. Clever? yes! When a man steals a loaf we cry down the knavery — when a man diverts his neighbour's mill-stream to grind his own corn, we cry up the cleverness! — And every one courts Captain Dudley Smooth!

Sir John. Why, who could offend him? — the best-bred, civillest creature — and a dead shot! There is not a cleverer man in the three kingdoms.

Eve. A study — a study! — let me examine him! Such men are living satires on the world.

Smooth passing his arm caressingly over SIR JOHN's *shoulder*]. My dear John, how well you are looking! A new lease of life! Introduce me to Mr. Evelyn.

Eve. Sir, it's an honour I've long ardently desired.
[*They bow and shake hands.*]

Enter SIR FREDERICK BLOUNT.

Blount. How d'ye do, Sir John? Ah, Evelyn — I wished so much to see you.

Eve. 'Tis my misfortune to be visible!

Blount. A little this way. You know, perhaps, that I once paid my addwesses to Miss Vesey; but since that vewy eccentwic will Sir John has shuffled me off, and hints at a pwior attachment — [*aside*] which I know to be false.

Eve. [*seeing* CLARA]. A prior attachment! — (Ha! Clara!) Well, another time, my dear Blount.

Enter CLARA.

Blount. Stay a moment — I want you to do me a favour with regard to Miss Douglas.

Eve. Miss Douglas!

Blount. Yes;— you see, though Georgina has gweat expectations, and Stingy Jack will leave her all that he has, yet she has only her legacy of £ 10,000 at the moment — no doubt closely settled on herself too: Clawa has £ 20,000. And, I think, Clawa always liked me a little.

Eve. You! I dare say she did!

Blount. It is whispered about that you mean to pwopose to Georgina. Nay, Sir John more than hinted that was her pwior attachment!

Eve. Indeed!

Blount. Now, as you are all in all with the family, if you could say a word for me to Miss Douglas, I don't see what harm it could do me! — [*Aside.*] I will punish Georgina for her pwerfidy.

Eve. 'Sdeath, man! speak for yourself! you are just the sort of man for young ladies to like — they understand you — you're of their own level. Pshaw! you're too modest — you want no mediator!

Blount. My dear fellow, you flatter me. I'm well enough in my way. But you, you know, would cawwy evewything before you! — you're so confoundedly wich!

Eve. [*turning to* CLARA]. Miss Douglas, what do you think of Sir Frederick Blount? Observe him. He is well dressed — young — tolerably handsome — (BLOUNT *bowing*) bows with an air — has plenty of small-talk — every thing to captivate. Yet he thinks that, if he and

I were suitors to the same lady, I should be more successful because I am richer. — What say you! Is love an auction? — and *do* women's hearts go to the highest bidder?

Clara. Their hearts? — No.

Eve. But their hands — yes! You turn away. Ah, you dare not answer that question!

Geor. [*aside*]. Sir Frederick flirting with Clara? I'll punish him for his perfidy. *You* are the last person to talk so, Mr. Evelyn! — you, whose wealth is your smallest attraction — you, whom every one admires — so witty, such taste, such talent! Ah, I'm very foolish!

Sir John [*clapping him on the shoulder*]. You must not turn my little girl's head. Oh, you're a sad fellow! Apropos, I must show you Georgina's last drawings. She has wonderfully improved since you gave her lessons in perspective.

Geor. No, papa! — No, pray, no! Nay, don't!

Sir John. Nonsense, child! — it's very odd, but she's more afraid of you than of any one!

Smooth [*to* BLOUNT *taking snuff*]. He's an excellent father, our dear John! and supplies the place of a mother to her.

[*Turns away to* LADY FRANKLIN *and* GRAVES.

> EVELYN *and* GEORGINA *seat themselves, and look over the drawings;* SIR JOHN *leans over them;* SIR FREDERICK *converses with* CLARA; EVELYN *watching them.*

Eve. Beautiful! — a view from Tivoli. (Death! — she looks down while he speaks to her!) Is there a little fault in that colouring? (She positively blushes!) But this Jupiter is superb. (What a d — d coxcomb it is!) [*Rising.*] Oh, she certainly loves him — I too can be loved elsewhere — I too can see smiles and blushes on the face of another.

Geor. Are you not well?

Eve. I beg pardon. Yes, you are indeed improved! Ah, who so accomplished as Miss Vesey?

[*Takes up the drawing; pays her marked attention in dumb show.*]

Clara. Yes, Sir Frederick, the concert was very crowded. Ah, I see that Georgina consoles him for the past! He has only praises for her, nothing but taunts for me!

Blount. I wish you would take my opewa-box next Saturday — 'tis the best in the house. I'm not wich, but I spend what I have on myself! I make a point to have evewything the best in a quiet way. Best opewa-box — best dogs — best horses — best house of its kind. I want nothing to complete my establishment but the best wife!

Clara [*abstractedly*]. That will come in good time, Sir Frederick.

Eve. Oh, it will come — will it? Georgina refused the trifler — *she* courts him [*taking up a portrait*]. Why, what is this? — my own —

Geor. You must not look at that — you must not, indeed. I did not know it was there.

Sir John. Your own portrait, Evelyn! Why, child, I was not aware you took likenesses: — that's something new. Upon my word it's a strong resemblance.

Geor. Oh, no — it does not do him justice. Give it to me. I will tear it. [*Aside.*] That odious Sir Frederick!

Eve. Nay, you shall not.

Clara. So — so — he loves her, then! Misery — misery! But he shall not perceive it! No — no — I can be proud too. Ha! ha! — Sir Frederick — excellent — excellent — you are so entertaining — ha! ha! [*laughs hysterically*].

Eve. Oh, the affectation of coquets — they cannot even laugh naturally!

    [CLARA *looks at him reproachfully, and walks aside with* SIR FREDERICK.

But where is the new guitar you meant to buy, Miss Vesey — the one inlaid with tortoiseshell? It is nearly a year since you set your heart on it, and I don't see it yet!

Sir John [*taking him aside confidentially*]. The guitar — oh, to tell you a secret — she applied the money I gave her for it to a case of charity several months ago — the very day the will was read. I saw the letter lying on the table, with the money in it. Mind, not a word to her — she'd never forgive me!

Eve. Letter!—money! What was the name of the person she relieved? — not Stanton?

Sir John. I don't remember, indeed.

Eve. [*taking out the letter*]. This is not her hand!

Sir John. No! I observed at the time it was not her hand, but I got out from her that she did not wish the thing to *be known,* and had employed some one else to copy it. May I see the letter? Yes, I think this is the wording. But I did not mean to tell you what case of charity it was. I promised Georgy I would not. Still, how did she know Mrs. Stanton's address? — you never gave it to me!

Eve. I gave it to her, Sir John.

Clara [*at the distance*]. Yes, I'll go to the opera, if Lady Franklin will. Do go, dear Lady Franklin! — on Saturday, then, Sir Frederick. [*Exit* BLOUNT.

Eve. Sir John, to a man like me, this simple act of unostentatious generosity is worth all the accomplishments in the world. A good heart — a tender disposition — a charity that shuns the day — a modesty that blushes at its own excellence — an impulse towards something more divine than Mammon; — such are the true accomplishments which preserve beauty for ever young. Such I have sought in the partner I would take for life; — such have I found — alas! not where I had dreamed! — Miss Vesey, I will be honest — I say then, frankly — [*as* CLARA *approaches, raising his voice and looking fixedly at her*] — I have loved another — deeply — truly — bitterly — *vainly!* I cannot offer to you, as I did to her, the fair first love of the human heart — rich with all its blossoms and its verdure. But if esteem — if gratitude — if an earnest resolve to conquer every recollection that would wander from your image; — if these can tempt you to accept my hand and fortune, my life shall be a study to deserve your confidence.

> [CLARA *stands motionless, clasping her hands, and then slowly seats herself.*

Sir John. The happiest day of my life!

> [CLARA *falls back in her chair.*

Eve. [*darting forward*]. [*Aside.*] She is pale; she faints! What have I done? Oh heaven! — Clara!

Clara [*rising with a smile*]. Be happy, my cousin — be happy! Yes, with my whole heart I say it — be happy, Alfred Evelyn!

ACT III. — SCENE I.

The drawing-rooms in Sir John Vesey's *house.*

Sir John, Georgina.

Sir John. And he has not pressed you to fix the wedding-day?

Geor. No; and since he proposed he comes here so seldom, and seems so gloomy. Heigho! Poor Sir Frederick was twenty times more amusing.

Sir John. But Evelyn is fifty times as rich!

Geor. Sir Frederick dresses so well!

Sir John. You'll have magnificent diamonds; but a word with you: I saw you yesterday in the square with Sir Frederick; that must not happen again. When a young lady is engaged to one man, nothing is so indecorous as to flirt with another. It might endanger your marriage itself. Oh, it's highly indecorous!

Geor. Don't be afraid, papa, — he takes up with Clara.

Sir John. Who, Evelyn?

Geor. Sir Frederick. Heigho! — I hate artful girls.

Sir John. The settlements will be splendid! if any-nothing can be handsomer than your

Geor. My own kind papa, you always put things so pleasantly. But do you not fear lest he discover that Clara wrote the letter?

Sir John. No; and I shall get Clara out of the house. But there is something else that makes me very uneasy. You know that no sooner did Evelyn come into possession of his fortune than he launched out in the style of a prince. His house in London is a palace, and he has bought a great estate in the country. Look how he lives! — Balls — banquets — fine arts — fiddlers — charities — and the devil to pay!

Geor. But if he can afford it —

Sir John. Oh! so long as he stopped *there* I had no apprehension; but since he proposed for you he is more extravagant than ever. They say he has taken to gambling: and he is always with Captain Smooth. No fortune can stand Deadly Smooth! If he gets into a scrape he may fall off from the settlements. We must press the marriage at once.

Geor. Heigho! Poor Frederick! You don't think he is *really* attached to Clara!

Sir John. Upon my word I can't say. Put on your bonnet, and come to Storr and Mortimer's to choose the jewels.

Geor. The jewels; — yes — the drive will do me good. So you'll send away Clara? — she's so very deceitful.

Sir John. Never fear — yes — tell her to come to me.

[*Exit* GEORGINA.

Yes! I must press on this marriage; Georgina has not wit enough to manage him — at least till he's her husband, and then all women find it smooth sailing. This match will make me a man of prodigious importance! I suspect he'll give me up her ten thousand pounds. I can't think of his taking to gambling, for I love him as a son — and I look on his money as my own.

SCENE II.

CLARA *and* SIR JOHN.

Sir John. Clara, my love!

Clara. Sir —

Sir John. My dear, what I am going to say may appear a little rude and unkind, but you know my character is frankness. — To the point then; my poor child, I am aware of your attachment to Mr. Evelyn —

Clara. Sir! *my attachment?*

Sir John. It is generally remarked. Lady Kind says you are falling away. My poor girl, I pity you — I do, indeed! Now, there's that letter you wrote to his old nurse — it has got about somehow — and the world is so ill-natured. I don't know if I did right; but after he had proposed to Georgy — (of course not before!) — I thought it so unpleasant for you, as a young lady, to be suspected of anything forward with respect to a man who was not attached to you, that I rather let it be supposed that Georgy *herself* wrote the letter.

Clara. Sir, I don't know what right you had to —

Sir John. That's very true, my dear: and I've been thinking since that I ought perhaps to tell Mr. Evelyn that the letter was yours — shall I?

Clara. No, sir; — I beg you will not. I — I — [*weeps*].

Sir John. My dear Clara, don't cry; I would not have said this for the world, if I was not a little anxious about my own girl. Georgina is so unhappy at what every one says of your attachment —

Clara. Every one? — Oh, torture!

Sir John. That it preys on her spirits — it even irritates her temper! You see, though the marriage will take place almost immediately, Mr. Evelyn does not come so often as he ought. In a word, I fear these little jealousies and suspicions will tend to embitter their future union. — I'm a father — forgive me.

Clara. Embitter their union! Oh, never! What would you have me do, sir?

Sir John. Why, you're now independent. Lady Franklin seems resolved to stay in town. Surely she can't mean to take her money out of the family by some foolish inclination for Mr. Graves? He is always purring and whining about the house, like a black cat in the megrims. What think you, eh?

Clara. Sir, it was of myself — my unhappy self, you were speaking.

Sir John. Sly! — True; true! What I meant to

say was this: — Lady Franklin persists in staying *here:* you are your own mistress. Mrs. Carlton, aunt to my late wife, is going abroad for a short time, and would be delighted if you would accompany her.

Clara. It is the very favour I would have asked of you. [*Aside.*] I shall escape at least the struggle and the shame. When does she go?

Sir John. In five days — next Monday. — You forgive me?

Clara. Sir, I thank you.

Sir John [*drawing the table*]. Suppose, then, you write a line to her yourself, and settle it at once?

Enter SERVANT.

Servant. The carriage, Sir John; Miss Vesey is quite ready.

Sir John. Wait a moment. SHALL I tell Evelyn you wrote the letter?

Clara. No, sir, I implore you.

Sir John. But it would be awkward for Georgy, if discovered.

Clara. It *never* shall be.

Sir John. Well, well, as you please. I know nothing could be so painful to a young lady of pride and delicacy. — James, if Mr. Serious, the clergyman, calls, say I'm gone to the great meeting at Exeter Hall: if Lord Spruce calls, say you believe I'm gone to the rehearsal of Cinderella. Oh! and if MacFinch should come — (Mac Finch, who duns me three times a week) — say I've hurried off to Garraway's to bid for the great Bulstrode estate. Just put the Duke of Lofty's card carelessly on the hall table. And I say, James, I expect two gentlemen a little before dinner — Mr. Squab the Radical, and Mr. Qualm of the great Marylebone Conservative Association. Show Squab into the study, and be sure to give him the "Weekly True Sun," — Qualm into the back parlour, with the "Times" and the "Morning Post." One must have a little management in this world. All humbug! — all humbug, upon my soul!

[*Exit.*

Clara [*folding the letter*]. There -- it is decided! A few days, and we are parted for ever! — a few weeks, and another will bear his name — his wife! Oh, happy fate! She will have the right to say to him — though the whole world should hear her — "I am thine!" And I embitter their lot — I am the cloud upon their joyous sunshine! And yet, O Alfred! if she loves thee — if she knows thee — if she values thee — and, when thou wrong'st her, if she can forgive, as I do — I can bless her when far away, and join her name in my prayer for thee!

Eve. [*without*]. Miss Vesey just gone? Well, I will write a line.

SCENE III.

EVELYN and CLARA.

Eve. [*aside*]. So — Clara! Do not let me disturb you, Miss Douglas.

Clara [*going*]. Nay, I have done.

Eve. I see that my presence is always odious to you, it is a reason why I come so seldom. But be cheered, madam: I am here but to fix the day of my marriage, and I shall then go into the country — till — till — In short, this is the last time my visit will banish you from the room I enter.

Clara [*aside*]. The last time! — and we shall then meet no more! — And to part thus for ever — in scorn — in anger — I cannot bear it! [*Approaching him.*] Alfred, my cousin, it is true, this may be the last time we shall meet — I have made my arrangements to quit England.

Eve. To quit England?

Clara. But before I go let me thank you for many a past kindness, which it is not for an orphan easily to forget.

Eve. [*mechanically*]. To quit England!

Clara. I have long wished it: but enough of me. — Evelyn, now that you are betrothed to another — now, without recurring to the past — now, without the fear of mutual error and mistake — something of our old friendship may at least return to us. — And if, too, I dared, I have that on my mind which only a friend — a sister — might presume to say to you.

Eve. [*moved*]. Miss Douglas — Clara — if there is ought that I could do — if, while hundreds — strangers — beggars tell me that I have the power, by opening or shutting this worthless hand, to bid sorrow rejoice, or poverty despair — if — if my life — my heart's blood — could render to *you* one such service as my gold can give to others — why, speak! — and the past you allude to — yes, even that bitter past — I will cancel and forget.

Clara [*holding out her hand*]. We are friends, then! you are again my cousin! my brother.

Eve. [*dropping her hand*]. Brother! Ah! say on!

Clara. I speak, then, as a sister — herself weak, inexperienced, ignorant, nothing — *might* speak to a brother, in whose career she felt the ambition of a man. Oh, Evelyn, when you inherited this vast wealth I pleased myself with imagining how you would wield the power delegated to your hands. I knew your benevolence — your intellect — your genius! — the ardent mind couched beneath the cold sarcasm of a long-baffled spirit! I saw before me the noble and bright career open to you at last — and I often thought that, in after-years, when far away — as I soon shall be — I should hear your name identified, not with what fortune can give the base, but with deeds and ends to which, for the *great*, fortune is but the instrument; — I often thought that I should say to my own heart — weeping proud and delicious tears — "And once this man loved me!"

Eve. No more, Clara! — oh, Heavens! — no more!

Clara. But *has* it been so? — have you been true to your own self? — Pomp — parade — luxuries — pleasures — follies! — all these might distinguish others — they do but belie the ambition and the soul of Alfred Evelyn! — Oh! pardon me — I am too bold — I pain — I offend you. Ah, I should not have dared thus much had I not thought at times, that — that —

Eve. That these follies — these vanities — this dalliance with a loftier fate were your own work! You thought that, and you were right! Perhaps, indeed, after a youth steeped to the lips in the hyssop and gall of penury — perhaps I might have wished royally to know the full value of that dazzling and starry life which, from the last step in the ladder, I had seen indignantly and from afar. But a month — a week would have sufficed for that experience. Experience! — Oh, how soon we learn that hearts are as cold and souls as vile — no matter whether the sun shine on the noble in his palace, or the rain drench the rags of the beggar cowering at the porch. The extremes of life differ but in this: — Above, *Vice* smiles and revels — below, *Crime* frowns and starves. But you — did not you reject me because I was poor? Despise me if you please! — my revenge might be unworthy — I wished to show you the luxuries, the gaud, the splendour I thought you prized, — to surround with the attributes your sex seems most to value the station that, had you loved me, it would have been yours to command. But vain — vain alike my poverty and my wealth! You loved me not in either, and my fate is sealed!

Clara. A happy fate, Evelyn! — you love!

'Eve. And at last I am beloved. [*After a pause, and turning to her abruptly.*] Do you doubt it?

Clara. No, I believe it firmly! — [*Aside.*] Were it possible for her not to love him?

Eve. Georgina, perhaps, is vain — and light — and —

Clara. No — think it not! Once removed from the worldly atmosphere of her father's counsels, and you will form and raise her to your own level. She is so young yet — she has beauty, cheerfulness, and temper; — the rest you will give, if you will but yet do justice to your own nature. And, now that there is nothing unkind between us — not even regret — and surely [*with a smile*] not revenge, my cousin, you will rise to your nobler self — and so, farewell!

Eve. No; stay, one moment; — you still feel interest in my fate! Have I been deceived? Oh why — why did you spurn the heart whose offerings were lavished at your feet? Could you still — still —? Distraction — I know not what I say: — my honour pledged to another — my vows accepted and returned! Go, Clara, it is best so! Yet you will miss some one, perhaps, more than me — some one to whose follies you have been more indulgent — some one to whom you would permit a yet tenderer name than that of brother!

Clara [*aside*]. It will make him, perhaps, happier to think it! Think so, if you will! — but part friends.

Eve. Friends — and that is all! Look you, this is life! The eyes that charmed away every sorrow — the hand whose lightest touch thrilled to the very core — the presence that, like moonlight, shed its own hallowing beauty over the meanest things; a little while — a year — a month — a day, and we smile that we could dream so idly. All — all — the sweet enchantment, known but once, never to return again, vanished from the world! And the one who forgets the soonest — the one who robs your earth for ever of its summer — comes to you with a careless lip, and says — "Let us part friends!" — Go, Clara, — go, — and be happy if you can!

Clara [*weeping*]. Cruel — cruel — to the last! — Heaven forgive you, Alfred! [*Exit.*

Eve. Soft! let me recall her words, her tones, her looks. — *Does she love me?* She defends her rival — she did not deny it when I charged her with attachment to another; and yet — and yet — there is a voice at my heart which tells me I have been the rash slave of a jealous anger. — But I have made my choice — I must abide the issue!

Enter GRAVES, *preceded by* Servant.

Ser. Lady Franklin is dressing, sir.

SCENE IV.

GRAVES and EVELYN.

Graves. Well, I'll wait. [*Exit* Servant.] She was worthy to have known the lost Maria! So considerate to ask me hither — not to console me, *that* is impossible — but to indulge the luxury of woe. It will be a mournful scene. — [*Seeing* EVELYN.] — Is that you, Evelyn? — I have just heard that the borough of Groginhole is vacant at last. Why not stand yourself? — with your property you might come in without even a personal canvass.

Eve. I, who despise these contests for the colour of a straw — this everlasting litigation of Authority *versus* Man — I to be one of the wranglers? — never!

Graves. You are quite right, and I beg your pardon.

Eve. [*Aside*]. And yet Clara spoke of ambition. She would regret me if I could be distinguished. — [*Aloud.*] To be sure, after all, Graves, corrupt as mankind are, it is our duty to try at least to make them a little better. An Englishman owes something to his country.

Graves. He does, indeed! [*counting on his fingers.*] East winds, Fogs, Rheumatism, Pulmonary Complaints, and Taxes — [EVELYN *walks about in disorder*]. You seem agitated — a quarrel with your intended? Oh!

when you've been married a month, you'll not know what to do without one!

Eve. You are a pleasant comforter.

Graves. Do you deserve a comforter? One morning you tell me you love Clara, or at least detest her, which is the same thing (poor Maria often said she detested *me*) — and that very afternoon you propose to Georgina!

Eve. Clara will easily console herself — thanks to Sir Frederick!

Graves. He is young!

Eve. Good looking!

Graves. A coxcomb!

Eve. And therefore irresistible!

Graves. Nevertheless, Clara has had the bad taste to refuse him. I have it from Lady Franklin, to whom he confided his despair in re-arranging his neck cloth!

Eve. My dear friend — is it possible?

Graves. But what then? You *must* marry Georgina, who, to believe Lady Franklin, is sincerely attached to — your fortune. Go and hang yourself, Evelyn; you have been duped by them.

Eve. By them — bah! If deceived, I have been my own dupe. Is it not a strange thing that in matters of reason — of the arithmetic and logic of life — we are sensible, shrewd, prudent men; but touch our hearts — move our passions — take us for an instant from the hard safety of worldly calculation — and the philosopher is duller than the fool? *Duped* — if I thought it! —

Graves. To be sure! — you tried Clara in your *poverty*; it was a safe experiment to try Georgina in your *wealth.*

Eve. Ha! that is true — very true. Go on.

Graves. You'll have an excellent father-in-law. Sir John positively weeps when he talks of your income!

Eve. Sir John, possibly — but Georgina?

Graves. Plays affection to you in the afternoon, after practising first with Sir Frederick in the morning.

Eve. On your life, sir, be serious: what do you mean?

Graves. That in passing this way I see her very often walking in the square with Sir Frederick.

Eve. Ha! say you so?

Graves. What then? Man is born to be deceived. You look nervous — your hand trembles; that comes of gaming. They say at the clubs that you play deeply.

Eve. Ha! ha! Do they say that? — a few hundreds lost or won — a cheap opiate — anything that can lay the memory to sleep. The poor man drinks, and the rich man gambles — the same motive to both! But you are right — it is a base resource — I will play no more.

Graves. I am delighted to hear it, for your friend Captain Smooth has ruined half the young heirs in London. To play with him is to advertise yourself a bankrupt. Even Sir John is alarmed. I met him just now in Pall Mall; he made me stop, and implored me to speak to you. By the by, I forgot — do you bank with Flash, Brisk, Credit, and Co.?

Eve. So, Sir John is alarmed? — [*Aside.*] Gulled by this cogging charlatan? — Aha! I may beat him yet at his own weapons! — Humph! Bank with Flash! Why do you ask me?

Graves. Because Sir John has just heard that they are in a very bad way, and begs you to withdraw anything you have in their hands.

Eve. I'll see to it. So Sir John is *alarmed* at my gambling?

Graves. Terribly! He even told me he should go himself to the club this evening, to watch you.

Eve. To watch me! — good — I will be there.

Graves. But you will promise not to play?

Eve. Yes — to play. I feel it is impossible to give it up!

Graves. No — no! 'Sdeath, man! be as wretched as you please; break your heart, that's nothing! but dammo, take care of your pockets.

Eve. I will be there — I will play with Captain Smooth — I will lose as much as I please — thousands — millions — billions; and if he presume to spy on my losses, hang me if I don't lose Sir John himself into the bargain! [*Going out and returning.*] I am so absent! What was the bank you mentioned? Flash, Brisk, and Credit? Bless me, how unlucky! and it's too late to draw out to-day. Tell Sir John I'm very much obliged to him, and he'll find me at the club any time before day-break, hard at work with my friend Smooth!

[*Exit.*

Graves. He's certainly crazy! but I don't wonder at it. What the approach of the dog-days is to the canine species, the approach of the honeymoon is to the human race.

Enter Servant.

Ser. Lady Franklin's compliments — she will see you in the *boudoir*, sir.

Graves. In the *boudoir!* — go, go — I'll come directly. [*Exit* Servant.

My heart beats — it must be for grief. Poor Maria! [*Searching his pockets for his handkerchief.*] Not a white one! — just like my luck: I call on a lady to talk of the dear departed, and I've nothing about me but a cursed gaudy, flaunting, red, yellow, and blue abomination from India, which it's even indecent for a disconsolate widower to exhibit. Ah! Fortune never ceases to torment the susceptible. The *boudoir!* — ha! ha! the *boudoir!* [*Exit.*

SCENE V.

A Boudoir in the same house.

Lady Frank. I take so much compassion on this poor man, who is determined to make himself wretched, that I am equally determined to make him happy! Well, if my scheme does but succeed, he shall laugh, he shall sing, he shall — Mum! — here he comes!

Enter GRAVES.

Graves [*sighing*]. Ah, Lady Franklin!

Lady Frank. [*sighing*]. Ah, Mr. Graves! [*They seat themselves.*] Pray excuse me for having kept you so long. Is it not a charming day?

Graves. An east wind, ma'am! but nothing comes amiss to you! — it's a happy disposition! Poor Maria! *she*, too, was naturally gay.

Lady Frank. Yes, she was gay. So much life, and a great deal of spirit.

Graves. Spirit? Yes! — nothing could master it. She *would* have her own way! Ah! there was nobody like her!

Lady Frank. And then, when her spirit was up, she looked so handsome! Her eyes grew so brilliant!

Graves. Did not they? — Ah! ah! ha! ha! ha! And do you remember her pretty trick of stamping her foot? — the tiniest little foot — I think I see her now. Ah! this conversation is very soothing!

Lady Frank. How well she acted in your private theatricals!

Graves. You remember her Mrs. Oakley, in "The Jealous Wife?" Ha! ha! how good it was! — ha! ha!

Lady Frank. Ha! ha! Yes, in the very first scene, when she came out with [*mimicking*] "Your unkindness and barbarity will be the death of me!"

Graves. No — no! that's not it! more energy. [*Mimicking.*] "Your unkindness and barbarity will be the DEATH of me." Ha! ha! I ought to know how she said it, for she used to practise it on me twice a-day. Ah! poor dear lamb! [*Wipes his eyes.*]

Lady Frank. And then she sang so well! was such a composer! What was that little French air she was so fond of?

Graves. Ha! ha! sprightly? was it not? Let me see — let me see.

Lady Frank. [*humming*]. Tum ti—ti tum—ti—ti—ti. No, that's not it.

Graves [*humming*]. Tum ti—ti—tum ti—ti—tum—tum—tum.

Both. Tum ti—ti—tum ti—ti—tum—tum—tum. Ha! ha!

Graves [*throwing himself back*]. Ah! what recollections it revives! It is too affecting.

Lady Frank. It *is* affecting; but we are all mortal. [*Sighs.*] And at your Christmas party at Cyprus Lodge, do you remember her dancing the Scotch reel with Captain Macnaughten?

Graves. Ha! ha! ha! To be sure — to be sure.

Lady Frank. Can you think of the step? — somehow thus, was it not? [*Dancing.*]

Graves. No — no — quite wrong! — just stand there. Now then [*humming the tune*]. — La — la-la-la. — La la, &c. [*They dance.* That's it — excellent — admirable!

Lady Frank. [*aside.*] Now it's coming.

Enter Sir John, Blount, Georgina,—*they stand amazed.*
  [Lady Franklin *continues to dance.*
  Graves. Bewitching — irresistible! It's Maria herself that I see before me! Thus — thus — let me clasp — Oh, the devil! Just like my luck! — [*Stopping opposite* Sir John]. Lady Franklin *runs off.*
  Sir John. Upon *my* word, Mr. Graves!
  Geor. Blount. Encore — encore! Bravo — bravo!
  Graves. It's all a mistake! I — I — Sir John. Lady Franklin, you see — that is to say — I — Sainted Maria! you are spared, at least, this affliction!
  Geor. Pray go on!
  Blount. Don't let us interrupt you.
  Graves. Interrupt me! I must say that this rudeness — this gross impropriety — to pry into the sorrows of a poor bereaved sufferer, seeking comfort from a sympathising friend — But such is human nature!
  Geor. But, Mr. Graves! — [*following him*].
  Graves. Heartless!
  Blount. My dear Mr. Graves! — [*following him*].
  Graves. Frivolous!
  Sir John. Stay and dine! — [*following him*].
  Graves. Unfeeling!
  Omnes. Ha! — ha! — ha!
  Graves. Monsters! Good day to you.*
    [*Exit, followed by* Sir John, *&c.*

* For the original idea of this scene the author is indebted to a little proverbs, never, he believes, acted in public.

SCENE VI.

The interior of * * * *'s *Club; night; lights, &c. Small sofa-tables, with books, papers, tea, coffee, &c. Several Members grouped by the fireplace; one Member with his legs over the back of his chair; another with his legs over his table; a third with his legs on the chimney-piece. To the left, and in front of the Stage, an old Member reading the newspaper, seated by a small round table; to the right a card-table, before which* CAPTAIN DUDLEY SMOOTH *is seated, and sipping lemonade; at the bottom of the Stage another card-table.*

GLOSSMORE *and* STOUT.

Gloss. You don't come often to the club, Stout?

Stout. No; time is money. An hour spent at a club is unproductive capital.

Old Mem. [*reading the newspaper*]. Waiter! — the snuffbox. [*Waiter brings it.*

Gloss. So, Evelyn has taken to play? I see Deadly Smooth, "hushed in grim repose, awaits his evening prey." Deep work to-night, I suspect, for Smooth is drinking lemonade — keeps his head clear — monstrous clever dog!

Enter EVELYN; *salutes and shakes hands with different members in passing up the Stage.*

How d'ye do, Glossmore? How are you, Stout? you don't play, I think? Political Economy never plays at cards, eh? — never has time for anything more frivolous than Rents and Profits, Wages and Labour, High Prices, and Low — Corn-Laws, Poor-Laws, Tithes, Currency — Dot-and-go-one — Rates, Puzzles, Taxes, Riddles, and Botheration! Smooth is the man. Aha! Smooth. Piquet, eh? You owe me my revenge!

[*Members touch each other significantly;* STOUT *walks away with the snuff-box;* Old Member *looks at him savagely.*

Smooth. My dear Alfred, anything to oblige.

[*They seat themselves.*

Old Mem. Waiter! — the snuff-box.

[Waiter *takes it from* STOUT *and brings it back to* Old Member.

Enter BLOUNT.

Blount. So, so! Evelyn at it again, — eh, Glossmore?

Gloss. Yes, Smooth sticks to him like a leech. Clever fellow, that Smooth!

Blount. Will you make up a wubber?

Gloss. Have you got two others?

Blount. Yes; Flat and Green.

Gloss. Bad players.

Blount. I make it a wule to play with bad players; it is five per cent. in one's favour. I hate gambling. But a quiet wubber, if one is the best player out of four, can't do one any harm.

Gloss. Clever fellow, that Blount!

[BLOUNT *takes up the snuff-box and walks off with it;* Old Member *looks at him savagely.*

[BLOUNT, GLOSSMORE, FLAT, and GREEN, *make up a table at the bottom of the Stage.*

Smooth. A thousand pardons, my dear Alfred, — ninety repique — ten cards! — game!

Eve. [*passing a note to him*]. Game! Before we go on, one question. This is Thursday — how much do you calculate to win of me before Tuesday next?

Smooth. Ce cher Alfred! He is so droll!

Eve. [*writing in his pocket-book*]. Forty games a-night — four nights, minus Sunday — our usual stakes — that would be right, I think!

Smooth [*glancing over the account*]. Quite — if I win all — which is next to impossible.

Eve. It shall be possible to win twice as much, on one condition. Can you keep a secret?

Smooth. My dear Alfred, I have kept myself! I never inherited a farthing — I never spent less than £4,000 a-year — and I never told a soul how I managed it.

Eve. Hark ye, then — a word with you — [*they whisper*].

Old Mem. Waiter! — the snuff-box!

[Waiter *takes it from* BLOUNT, &c.

Enter SIR JOHN.

Eve. You understand?

Smooth. Perfectly; anything to oblige.

Eve. [*cutting*]. It is for you to deal.

[*They go on playing.*

Sir John [*groaning*]. There's my precious son-in-law, that is to be, spending *my* consequence, and making a fool of himself.

[*Takes up the snuff-box;* Old Member *looks at him savagely.*

Blount. I'm out. Flat, a poney on the odd twick. That's wight. — [*Coming up counting his money.*] Well, Sir John, you don't play!

Sir John. Play? no! Confound him — lost again!

Eve. Hang the cards! — double the stakes!

Smooth. Just as you please — done!

Sir John. Done, indeed!

Old Mem. Waiter! — the snuff-box.

[Waiter *takes it from* Sir John.

Blount. I've won eight points and the bets — I never lose — I never play in the Deadly Smooth set!

[*Takes up the snuff-box;* Old Member *as before.*

Sir John [*looking over* Smooth's *hand, and fidgetting backwards and forwards*]. Lord, have mercy on us! Smooth has seven for his point! What's the stakes?

Eve. Don't disturb us — I only throw out four. Stakes, Sir John? — immense! Was ever such luck? — not a card for my point. Do stand back, Sir John — I'm getting irritable.

Old Mem. Waiter! the snuff-box.

[Waiter *brings it back.*

Blount. One hundred pounds on the next game, Evelyn?

Sir John. Nonsense — nonsense — don't disturb him! All the fishes come to the bait! Sharks and minnows all nibbling away at my son-in-law!

Eve. One hundred pounds, Blount? Ah! the finest gentleman is never too fine a gentleman to pick up a guinea. Done! Treble the stakes, Smooth!

Sir John. I'm on the rack! [*seizing the snuff-box*]. Be cool, Evelyn! take care, my dear boy! Be cool — be cool.

Eve. What — what? You have four queens! — five to the king. Confound the cards! a fresh pack. [*Throws the cards behind him over* SIR JOHN.]

Old Mem. Waiter! the snuff-box.

[*Different members gather round.*

First Mem. I never before saw Evelyn out of temper. He must be losing immensely!

Second Mem. Yes, this is interesting!

Sir John. Interesting! There's a wretch!

First Mem. Poor fellow! he'll be ruined in a month!

Sir John. I'm in a cold sweat.

Second Mem. Smooth is the very devil.

Sir John. The devil's a joke to him!

Gloss. [*slapping* SIR JOHN *on the back*]. A clever fellow that Smooth, Sir John, eh? *Takes up the snuff-box.* Old Member *as before.*] £100 on this game, Evelyn?

Eve. [*half turning round*]. You! well done the Constitution! yes, £100!

Old Mem. Waiter! — the snuff-box.

Stout. I *think* I'll venture £200 on this game, Evelyn?

Eve. [*quite turning round*]. Ha! ha! ha! — Enlightenment and the Constitution on the same side of the question at last! Oh Stout, Stout! — greatest happiness of the greatest number — greatest number, number one Done, Stout! — £200! ha! ha! ha! — deal, Smooth. Well done, Political Economy — ha! ha! ha!

Sir John. Quite hysterical — drivelling! Ar'nt you ashamed of yourselves? His own cousins — all in a conspiracy — a perfect gang of them.

[*Members indignant.*

Stout. [*to Members*]. Hush! he's to marry Sir John's daughter.

First Mem. What, Stingy Jack's? oh!

Chorus of Mems. Oh! oh!

Old Mem. Waiter! the snuff-box.

Eve. [*rising in great agitation*]. No more, no more — I've done! — quite enough. Glossmore, Stout, Blount — I'll pay you to-morrow. I — I — Death! — this is ruinous!

[*Seizes the snuff-box;* Old Member *as before.*

Sir John. Ruinous? I dare say it is. What has he lost? what *has* he lost, Smooth? Not much? eh? eh?

[*Omnes gather round* Smooth.

Smooth. Oh, a trifle, dear John! — excuse me! We never tell our winnings. — [*To* BLOUNT.] How d'ye do, Fred? — [*To* GLOSSMORE.] By the by, Charles, don't you want to sell your house in Grosvenor Square? — £12,000, eh?

Gloss. Yes, and the furniture at a valuation. About £3,000 more.

Smooth [*looking over his pocket-book*]. Um! — Well, we'll talk of it.

Sir John. 12 and 3 — £15,000. What a cold-blooded rascal it is! — £15,000, Smooth?

Smooth. Oh, the house itself is a trifle; but the establishment — I'm considering whether I have enough to keep it up, my dear John.

Old Mem. Waiter, the snuff-box! [*Scraping it round, and with a wry face.*] — And it's all gone!

[*Gives it to the* Waiter *to fill.*

Sir John [*turning round*]. And it's all gone!

Eve. [*starting up and laughing hysterically*]. Ha! ha! all gone? not a bit of it. Smooth, this club is so noisy. Sir John, you are always in the way. Come to my house! come! Champagne and a broiled bone. Nothing venture, nothing have! The luck must turn, and by Jupiter we'll make a night of it!

Sir John. A night of it!!! For Heaven's sake, Evelyn! EVELYN!! — think what you are about! — think of Georgina's feelings! think of your poor lost mother! — think of the babes unborn! think of —

Eve. I'll think of nothing! Zounds! — you don't know what I have lost, man; it's all your fault, distracting my attention. Pshaw — pshaw! Out of the way, do! Come, Smooth. Ha! ha! a night of it, my boy — a night of it!
[*Exeunt* SMOOTH *and* EVELYN.

Sir John [*following*]. You must not, you shall not! Evelyn, my dear Evelyn! he's drunk — he's mad! Will no one send for the police?

Mems. Ha! ha! ha! Poor old stingy Jack!

Old Mem. [*rising for the first time, and in a great rage*]. Waiter! — the snuff-box!

ACT IV. — SCENE I.

The Ante-room in EVELYN'S *house, as in Scene I., Act II.*

TABOURET, MACFINCH, FRANTZ, *and other* Tradesmen.

Tabou. [*half whispers*]. So, I hear that Mr. Evelyn has turned gamester! There are strange reports about to-day — I don't know what to make of it! We must look sharp, Mr. Macfinch, we poor tradesmen, and make hay while the sun shines.

Macfinch. I wuish those geeming-houses were aw at the deevil! — It's a sheam and a sin for gentlemen to gang and ruin themselves, when we honest tradesmen could do it for them with sae muckle advantage to the arts and coummerce o' the country! [*Omnes shake their heads approvingly.*]

Enter SMOOTH *from the inner room, with a pocket-book and pencil in his hand.*

Smooth [*looking round*]. Hum! ha! Fine pictures! — [*Feeling the curtains.*] The new-fashioned velvet, hum! good proportioned rooms! Yes, this house is better than Glossmore's! Oh, Mr. Tabouret, the upholsterer! you furnished these rooms? All of the best, eh?

Tabou. Oh, the VERY best! Mr. Evelyn is not a man to grudge expense, sir!

Smooth. He is not, indeed. You've been paid, I suppose, Tabouret?

Tabou. No, sir, no — I never send in my bills when a customer is rich. [*Aside.*] Bills are like trees, and grow by standing.

Smooth. Humph! Not PAID? humph?

[*Omnes gather round.*

Macfinch. I dinna like that hoomph, there's something vara suspeecious abun' it.

Tabou. [*to the tradesmen*]. It is the great card-player, Captain Smooth — finest player in Europe — cleaned out the Duke of Sillyvale. Uncommoningly clever man!

Smooth [*pacing about the room*]. Thirty-six feet by twenty-eight — Um! I think a bow-window *there* would be an *improvement:* could it be done easily, Tabouret?

Macfinch. If Mr. Evelyn wants to pool about his house, there's no mon like my friend Mr. MacStucco.

Smooth. Evelyn! I was speaking of *myself.* Mr. MacStucco? — humph!

Tabou. Yourself? Have you bought the house, sir?

Smooth. Bought it? — hum! — ha! — it depends — So you've not been paid yet? — um! Nor you — nor you — nor you! Hum! ha!

Tabou. No, sir! — what *then?* No fear of Mr. EVELYN! Ha! ha!

Omnes [*anxiously*]. Ha! ha! — what then?

Macfinch. Ah, sir, what then? I'm a puir mon with a family; this way, Captain! You've a leetle account in the buiks; an' we'll e'en wipe it out altogether, gin you'll say what you mean by that Hoom ha!

Smooth. Macfinch, my dear fellow, don't oblige me to cane you; I would not have Mr. Evelyn distressed for the world. Poor fellow! he holds very bad cards. So you've not been paid yet? Don't send in your bills on any account — Mind! Yes; I don't dislike the house with some alteration. Good day to you — Hum! ha!

[*Exit, looking about him, examining the chairs, tables, &c.*

Tabou. Plain as a pike-staff! staked his very house on an odd trick!

SCENE II.

The foregoing. — Enter SHARP *from the inner room, agitated, and in a hurry.*

Sharp. O Lord! O Lord! — who'd have thought it? Cards are the devil's books! John! — Thomas! — Harris! — [*ringing the bell*].

Enter Two Servants.

Tom, take this letter to Sir John Vesey's. If not at home, find him — he will give you a cheque. Go to his banker's, and get it cashed *instantly*. Quick — quick! off with you!

Tabou. [*seizing* Servant]. What's the matter — what's the matter? How's Mr. Evelyn?

Ser. Bad — very bad! Sate up all night with Captain Smooth! [*Runs off.*

Sharp [*to the other* Servant]. Yes, Harris, your poor master! O dear! O dear! You will take this note to the Belgian minister, Portland-place. Passport for Ostend! Have the travelling carriage ready at a moment's notice!

Macfinch [*stopping* Servant]. Passport! Harkye, my mon; is he gaun to pit the saut seas between us and the siller?

Ser. Don't stop me — something wrong in the chest — change of air — late hours — and Captain Smooth! [*Exit.*

Sharp [*walking about*]. And if the bank should break! — if the bank *is* broke, and he can't draw out! — bound to Smooth.

Tabou. Bank! — what bank?

Sharp. Flash's bank! Flash, brother-in-law to Captain Smooth! What have *you* heard? — eh? — eh?

Tabou. That there's an awful run on it!

Sharp. I must be off. Go — go — you can't see Mr. Evelyn to-day!

Tabou. My account, sir!

Macfinch. I've a muckle bairns and a sma' bill!

Frantz. O sare, de great gentlemen always tink first of de tailor!

Sharp. Call again — call again at Christmas. The bank, — the cards, — the bank! O dear! O dear! [*Exit.*

Tabou. The bank!

Macfinch. The passport!

Frantz. And all dat vil be seen of de great Evelyn coat is de back of it! *Donner und Hagel!* — I vil arrest him — I vil put de salt on de tail of it!

Tabou. [*aside*]. I'll slip down to the city and see how the bank goes!

Macfinch [*aside*]. I'll e'en gang to my coosin the la'yer. Nothing but pcetience for us, Mr. Tabouret.

Tabou. Ay, ay, — stick by each other — share and share alike — that's my way, sir.

Omnes. Share and share alike.   [*Exeunt.*

SCENE III.

Enter Servant, GLOSSMORE, *and* BLOUNT.

Ser. My master is not very well, my lord! but I'll let him know.

[*Exit.*

Gloss. I am very curious to learn the result of his gambling tête-à-tête.

Blount. Oh, he's so howwidly wich, he can afford even a tête-à-tête with Deadly Smooth!

Gloss. Poor old Stingy Jack! why Georgina was *your* intended.

Blount. Yes; and I really liked the girl, though out of pique I pwoposed to her cousin. But what can a man do against money?

Enter EVELYN.

If we could start fair, you'd see whom Georgina would pwefer: but she's sacwificed by her father! She as much as told me so!

Eve. So, so, gentlemen, we've a little account to settle — one hundred each.

Both. Don't talk of it.

Eve. [*putting up his pocket-book*]. Well, I'll not talk of it! — [*Taking* BLOUNT *aside*]. Ha! ha! you'd hardly believe it — but I'd rather not pay you just at present: my money is locked up, and I must wait, you know, for the Groginhole rents. So, instead of owing you one hundred pounds, suppose I owe you *five?* You can give me a cheque for the other four. And, harkye! not a word to Glossmore.

Blount. Glossmore! the gweatest gossip in London! I shall be delighted! — [*Aside*]. It never does harm to lend to a wich man; one gets it back somehow. By the way, Evelyn, if you want my gwey cab-horse, you may have him for two hundwed pounds, and that will make seven.

Eve. [*aside*]. That's the fashionable usury: your friend does not take interest — he sells you a horse — [*Aloud*]. Blount, it's a bargain.

Blount [*writing the cheque, and musingly*]. No; I don't see what harm it can do me; that off-leg must end in a spavin.

Eve. [*to* GLOSSMORE]. That hundred pounds I owe you is rather inconvenient at present; I've a large sum to make up for the Groginhole property — perhaps you would lend me five or six hundred more — just to go on with?

Gloss. Certainly! Hopkins is dead: your interest for Cipher would —

Eve. Why, I can't promise *that* at this moment. But as a slight mark of friendship and gratitude, I shall be very much flattered if you'll accept a splendid grey cab-horse I bought to-day — cost two hundred pounds!

Gloss. Bought *to-day!* — then I'm safe. My dear fellow, you're always so princely!

Eve. Nonsense! just write the cheque; and, harkye, not a syllable to Blount!

Gloss. Blount! He's the town-crier! [*Goes to write.*

Blount [*giving* EVELYN *the cheque*]. Wansom's, Pall-mall East.

Eve. Thank you. So you *proposed* to Miss Douglas!

Blount. Hang it! yes; I could have sworn that she fancied me; her manner, for instance, that vewy day you pwoposed for Miss Vesey, otherwise Georgina —

Eve. Has only half what Miss Douglas has.

Blount. You forget how much Stingy Jack must have saved! But I beg your pardon.

Eve. Never mind; but not a word to Sir John, or he'll fancy I'm ruined.

Gloss. [*giving the cheque*]. Ransom's, Pall-mall East. Tell me, did you win or lose last night?

Eve. Win! lose! oh! No more of that, if you love

me. I must send off at once to the banker's [*looking at the two cheques*].

Gloss. [*aside*]. Why! he's borrowed from Blount, too!

Blount [*aside*]. That's a cheque from Lord Glossmore!

Eve. Excuse me; I must dress; I have not a moment to lose. You remember you dine with me to-day — seven o'clock. You'll meet Smooth. [*With tears in his voice*]. It may be the last time I shall ever welcome you here! My — what am I saying? — Oh, merely a joke! — good bye — *good* bye.

[*Shaking them heartily by the hand. Exit by the inner room.*

Blount. Glossmore!
Gloss. Blount!
Blount. I am afraid all's not wight!
Gloss. I incline to your opinion!
Blount. But I've sold my gwoy cab-horse.
Gloss. Grey cab-horse! you! What is he really worth now?
Blount. Since he is sold, I will tell you — Not a sixpence!
Gloss. Not a sixpence? he gave it to me!

[EVELYN *at the door giving directions to a* Servant *in dumb show.*

Blount. That was devilish unhandsome! Do you know, I feel nervous!

Gloss. Nervous! Let us run and stop payment of our cheques.

[EVELYN *shuts the door, and* Servant *runs across the stage.*

Blount. Hollo, John! where so fast?

Ser. [*in great haste*]. Beg pardon, Sir Frederick, to Pall-mall East — Messrs. Ransom.   [*Exit.*

Blount [*solemnly*]. Glossmore, we are fwoored?

Gloss. Sir, the whole town shall know of it. [*Exeunt.*

SCENE IV.

Enter TOKE *and other* Servants.

Toke. Come, come, stir yourselves! we've no time to lose. This room is to be got ready for the shawls. Mrs. Crump and the other ladies of the household are to wait here on the women before they go up to the drawing-room. Take away that desk: don't be lazy! and give me the newspaper.

[TOKE *seats himself; the* Servants *bustle about.*

Strange reports about my patron! and the walley is gone for the passport!

Enter FRANTZ *with a bundle.*

Frantz. Mr. Toke, my goot Mr. Toke, I've brought you von leetel present.

Toke. John and Charles vanish! [*Exeunt* Servants. I scorn to corrupt them 'ere working classes!

Frantz [*producing a pair of small-clothes which* TOKE *examines*]. Your master is von beggar! He vants to run avay; ve are all in de same vat-you-call-it — de same leetel nasty boat, Mr. Toke! Just let my friend Mr. Clutch up through the area. I vill put vat you call un execution on de gutes and de cattles dis very tay.

Toke. I accept the abridgements: but you've forgotten to line the pockets!

Frantz. Blesh my soul, so I have! [*giving a note*].

Toke. The area-gate shall be left undefended. Do it quietly, no *claw*, as the French say.

Frantz. Goot Mr. Toke — to-morrow I vill line de oter pocket. [*Exit.*

Toke. My patron does not give me satisfaction!

Enter Footman.

Foot. What chandeliers are to be lighted, Mr. Toke? — it's getting late.

Toke. Don't disturb me — I'm rum-mynating! — yes, yes, there's no doubt of it! Charles, the area-gate is open.

Foot. And all the plate in the pantry! I'll run and —

Toke. Not a stop! leave it open.

Foot. But —

Toke [*with dignity*]. "Tis for the sake of wentilation!
[*Exeunt.*

SCENE V.

A splendid saloon in EVELYN's *house.*

EVELYN *and* GRAVES.

Graves. You've withdrawn your money from Flash and Brisk?

Eve. No.

Graves. No! — then —

Enter SIR JOHN, LADY FRANKLIN, *and* GEORGINA.

Sir John. You got the cheque for £500 safely? — too happy to —

Eve. [*interrupting him*]. My best thanks! — my warmest gratitude! So kind in you! so seasonable! — that £500 — you don't know the value of that £500. I shall never forget your nobleness of conduct.

Sir John. Gratitude! Nobleness! — [*Aside.*] I can't have been taken in?

Eve. And in a moment of such distress!

Sir John [*aside*]. Such distress! He picks out the ugliest words in the whole dictionary!

Eve. I've done with Smooth. But I'm still a little crippled, and you must do me *another* favour. I've only as yet paid the deposit of ten per cent. for the great Groginhole property. I am to pay the rest this week — nay, I fear to-morrow. I've already sold out of the Funds! the money lies at the banker's, and of course I can't touch it; for if I don't pay by a certain day, I forfeit the estate and the deposit.

Sir John. What's coming now, I wonder?

Eve. Georgina's fortune is £ 10,000. I always meant, my dear Sir John, to present you with that little sum.

Sir John. Oh, Evelyn! your generosity is positively touching [*wipes his eyes*].

Eve. But the news of my losses has frightened my tradesmen! I have so many heavy debts at this moment that — that — that —. But I see Georgina is listening, and I'll say what I have to say to her.

Sir John. No, no — no, no. Girls don't understand business!

Eve. The very reason I speak to her. This is an affair not of business, but of *feeling*. Stout, show Sir John my Correggio.

Sir John [*aside*]. Devil take his Correggio! The man is born to torment me!

Eve. My dear Georgina, whatever you may hear said of me, I flatter myself that you feel confidence in my honour.

Geor. Can you doubt it?

Eve. I confess that I am embarrassed at this moment: I have been weak enough to lose money at play; and there are other demands on me. I promise you never to gamble again as long as I live. My affairs can be retrieved; but for the first few years of our marriage it may be necessary to retrench.

Geor. Retrench!

Eve. To live, perhaps, altogether in the country.

Geor. Altogether in the country!

Eve. To confine ourselves to a modest competence.

Geor. Modest competence! I knew something horrid was coming!

Eve. And now, Georgina, you may have it in your power at this moment to save me from much anxiety and humiliation. My money is locked up — my debts of honour must be settled — you are of age — your £10,000 in your own hands —

Sir John [STOUT *listening as well as* SIR JOHN]. I'm standing on hot iron!

Eve. If you could lend it to me for a few weeks — You hesitate! oh! believe the honour of the man you will call your husband before all the calumnies of the fools whom we call the world! Can you give me this proof of your confidence? Remember, without confidence what is wedlock?

Sir John [*aside to her*]. No! [*Aloud, pointing his glass at the Correggio.*] Yes, the painting may be fine.

Stout. But you don't like the subject?

Geor. [*aside*]. He may be only trying me! Best leave it to papa.

Eve. Well —

Geor. You — you shall hear from me to-morrow. — [*Aside.*] Ah, there's that dear Sir Frederick!

[*Goes to* BLOUNT.

Enter GLOSSMORE *and* SMOOTH; EVELYN *salutes them, paying* SMOOTH *servile respect.*

Lady Frank. [*to* GRAVES]. Ha! ha! To be so disturbed yesterday, — was it not droll?

Graves. Never recur to that humiliating topic.

Gloss. [*to* STOUT]. See how Evelyn fawns upon Smooth!

Stout. How mean in him! — *Smooth* — a professional gambler — a fellow who lives by his wits! I would not know such a man on any account!

Smooth [*to* GLOSSMORE]. So Hopkins is dead — you want Cipher to come in for Groginhole, eh?

Gloss. What! — could *you* manage it?

Smooth. Ce cher Charles! — anything to oblige!

Stout. Groginhole! What can he have to do with Groginhole? Glossmore, present me to Smooth.

Gloss. What! the gambler — the fellow who lives by his wits?

Stout. Why, his wits seem to be an uncommonly productive capital? I'll introduce myself. How d'ye do, Captain Smooth? We have met at the club, I think — I am charmed to make your acquaintance in private. I say, sir, what do you think of the affairs of the nation? Bad! very bad! — no enlightenment! — great fall off in the revenue! — no knowledge of finance! There's only one man who can save the country — and that's POPKINS!

Smooth. Is he in Parliament, Mr. Stout? What's your Christian name, by-the-bye?

Stout. Benjamin. — No; — constituencies are so ignorant, they don't understand his value. He's no orator: in fact, he stammers so much — but devilish profound. Could not we ensure him for Groginhole?

Smooth. My dear Benjamin, it is a thing to be thought on.

Eve. [*advancing*]. My friends, pray be seated; — I wish to consult you. This day twelve months I succeeded to an immense income, and as, by a happy coincidence, on the same day I secured your esteem, so now I wish to ask you if you think I could have spent that income in a way more worthy your good opinion.

Gloss. Impossible! excellent taste — beautiful house!

Blount. Vewy good horses — [*Aside to* GLOSSMORE] especially the gwey cab!

Lady Frank. Splendid pictures!

Graves. And a magnificent cook, ma'am!

Smooth [*thrusting his hands into his pockets*]. It is my opinion, Alfred — and I'm a judge — that you could not have spent your money better!

Omnes [*except* SIR JOHN]. Very true!

Eve. What say *you*, Sir John? You may think me a little extravagant; but you know that in this world the only way to show one's self thoroughly respectable is to make a thoroughly respectable show.

Sir John. Certainly — certainly! No, you could not have done better. [*Aside*]. I don't know what to make of it.

Geor. Certainly. — [*Coaxingly*]. Don't retrench, my dear Alfred!

Gloss. Retrench! nothing so plebeian!

Stout. Plebeian, sir! — worse than plebeian! — it is against all the rules of public morality. Every one knows, now-a-days, that extravagance is a benefit to the population — encourages art — employs labour — and multiplies spinning-jennies.

Eve. You reassure me! I own I did think that a man worthy of friends so sincere might have done something better than feast — dress — drink — play —

Gloss. Nonsense! — we like you the better for it. [*Aside*]. I wish I had my £600 back, though.

Eve. And you are as much my friends now as when you offered me £10 for my old nurse?

Sir John. A thousand times more so, my dear boy!

[*Omnes approve.*

Enter SHARP.

Smooth. But who's our new friend?

Eve. Who! the very man who first announced to me the wealth which you allow I have spent so well. But what's the matter, Sharp?

SHARP [*whispering* EVELYN].

Eve. [*aloud*]. The bank's *broke!*

Sir John. Broke! — what bank?

Eve. Flash, Brisk, and Co.

Gloss. [*to* SMOOTH]. And Flash was your brother-in-law. I'm very sorry.

Smooth [*taking snuff*]. Not at all, Charles, — I did not bank there.

Sir John. But I warned you — you withdrew?

Eve. Alas! no!

Sir John. Oh! Not much in their hands?

Eve. Why, I told you the purchase-money for Groginhole was at my bankers' — but no, no: don't look so frightened! It was not placed with Flash — it is at Hoare's — it is, indeed. Nay, I assure you it is. A mere trifle at Flash's, upon my word, now! To-morrow, Sharp, we'll talk of this! One day more — one day, at least, for enjoyment.

Sir John. Oh! a pretty enjoyment!

Blount. And he borrowed £700 of me!

Gloss. And £600 of me!

Sir John. And £500 of me!

Stout. Oh! a regular Jeremy Diddler!

Smooth [*to* SIR JOHN]. John, do you know, I think I would take a handsome offer for this house just as it stands — furniture, plate, pictures, books, bronzes, and statues!

Sir John. Powers above!

Stout [*to* SIR JOHN]. I say, you have placed your daughter in a very unsafe investment What then? — a daughter's like any other capital — transfer the stock in hand to t'other speculation.

Sir John [*going to* GEORGINA]. He! I'm afraid we've been very rude to Sir Frederick. A monstrous fine young man!

Enter TOKE.

Toke [*to* EVELYN]. Sir, I beg your pardon, but Mr. Macfinch insists on my giving you this letter instantly.

Eve. [*reading*]. How! Sir John, this fellow, Macfinch, has heard of my misfortunes, and insists on being paid, — a lawyer's letter — quite insolent!

Toke. And, sir, Mr. Tabouret is below, and declares he will not stir till he's paid.

Eve. Not stir till he's paid! What's to be done, Sir John? — Smooth, what *is* to be done?

Smooth. If he'll not stir till he's paid, make him up a bed, and I'll take him in the inventory, as one of the fixtures, Alfred!

Eve It is very well for you to joke, Mr. Smooth. But —

Enter Sheriff's Officer, *giving a paper to* EVELYN, *and whispering.*

Eve. What's this? Frantz, the tailor. Why, the impudent scoundrel! Faith, this is more than I bargained for — Sir John, the bailiffs are in the house!

Stout [*slapping* SIR JOHN *on the back with glee*]. The bailiffs are in the house, old gentleman! But I didn't lend him a farthing.

Eve. And for a mere song — £150! Sir John, pay this fellow, will you? or see that my people kick out the bailiffs, or do it yourself, or something, — while we go to dinner!

Sir John. Pay — kick — I'll be d—d if I do! — Oh, my £500! my £500! Mr. Alfred Evelyn, I want my £500!

Graves. I'm going to do a very silly thing — I shall lose both my friend and my money; — just like my luck! — Evelyn, go to dinner — I'll settle this for you.

Lady Frank. I love you for that!

Graves. Do you? then I am the happiest — Ah! ma'am, I don't know what I am saying!

[*Exeunt* GRAVES *and* Officer.

Eve. [*to* GEORGINA]. Don't go by these appearances! I repeat £10,000 will more than cover all my embarrassments. I shall hear from you to-morrow?

Geor. Yes — yes!

Eve. But you're not going? — You, too, Glossmore? — you, Blount? — you, Stout — you, Smooth?

Smooth. No; I'll stick by you as long as you've a guinea to stake!

Gloss. Oh, this might have been expected from a man of such ambiguous political opinions!

Stout. Don't stop me, sir. No man of common enlightenment would have squandered his substance in this way. Pictures and statues? — baugh!

Eve. Why, you all said I could not spend my money better! Ha! ha! ha! — the absurdest mistake!

—you don't fancy I'm going to prison? — Ha! ha! — Why don't you laugh, Sir John? — Ha! ha! ha!

Sir John. Sir, this horrible levity! — Take Sir Frederick's arm, my poor, injured, innocent child! — Mr. Evelyn, after this extraordinary scene, you can't be surprised that I — I — Zounds! I'm suffocating!

Smooth. But, my dear John, it is for us at least to put an execution on the dinner.

Stout [*aside*]. The election at Groginhole is tomorrow. This news may not arrive before the poll closes. — [*Rushing to* EVELYN.] Sir, Popkins never bribes: but Popkins will bet you £1,000 that he don't come in for Groginhole.

Gloss. This is infamous, Mr. Stout! Cipher is a man who scorns every subterfuge! — [*Aside to* EVELYN.] But, for the sake of the Constitution, name your price.

Eve. I know the services of Cipher — I know the profundity of Popkins; but it is too late — the borough's engaged!

Toke. Dinner is served.

Gloss. [*pausing*]. Dinner!

Stout. Dinner! a very good smell!

Eve. [*to* SIR JOHN]. Turtle and venison too. [*They stop irresolute.*

Eve. That's right — come along. But, I say, Blount — Stout — Glossmore — Sir John — one word first; will you lend me £10 for my old nurse?
[*They all fall back.*

Ah! you fall back. — Behold a lesson for all who build friendship upon their fortune, and not their virtues! — You lent me hundreds this morning to squander upon pleasure — you would refuse me £10 now to bestow upon benevolence. Go — we have done with each other — go!

[*Exeunt, indignantly, all but* EVELYN *and* SMOOTH.

Re-enter GRAVES.

Graves. Heyday! — what's all this?

Eve. Ha! ha! — the scheme prospers — the duper is duped! Come, my friends — come: when the standard of money goes down, in the great battle between man and fate — why, a bumper to the brave hearts that refuse to desert us. [*Exeunt.*

ACT V. — SCENE I.

*****'s *Club;* SMOOTH, GLOSSMORE — *other Members.*

Gloss. Will his horses be sold, think you?

Smooth. Very possibly, Charles! — a fine stud — hum! — ha! Waiter, a glass of sherry!

Gloss. They say he must go abroad!

Smooth. Well; 'tis the best time of year for travelling, Charles!

Gloss. We are all to be paid to-day; and that looks suspicious!

Smooth. Very suspicious, Charles! Hum! — ah!

Gloss. My dear fellow, you must know the rights of the matter: I wish you'd speak out. What have you really won? Is the house itself gone?

Smooth. The house itself is certainly not gone, Charles, for I saw it exactly in the same place this morning at halfpast ten — it has not moved an inch.

[Waiter *gives a letter to* GLOSSMORE.

Gloss. [reading]. From Groginhole — an express! What's this? I'm amazed! ! ! [*Reading.*] "They've actually, at the eleventh hour, started Mr. Evelyn; and nobody knows what his politics are! We shall be beat! — the Constitution is gone! — CIPHER!" Oh!

this is infamous in Evelyn! Gets into Parliament just
to keep himself out of the Bench.
Smooth. He's capable of it.
Gloss. Not a doubt of it, sir! — Not a doubt of it!

Enter SIR JOHN *and* BLOUNT, *talking.*

Sir John. My dear boy, I'm not flint! I am but a
man! If Georgina really loves you — and I am sure
that she *does* — I will never think of sacrificing her
happiness to ambition — she is yours: I told her so
this very morning.
Blount [aside]. The old humbug!
Sir John. She's the best of daughters! — the most
obedient, artless creature! Oh! she's been properly
brought up! a good daughter makes a good wife.
Dine with me at seven, and we'll talk of the settlements.
Blount. Yes; I don't care for fortune; — but —
Sir John. Her £10,000 will be settled on herself
— that of course.
Blount. All of it, sir? Weally, I —
Sir John. What *then*, my dear boy? I shall leave
you both all I've laid by. Ah! you know I'm a close
fellow! "Stingy Jack," — eh? After all, worth makes
the man!
Smooth. And the more a man's worth, John, the
worthier man he must be.   [*Exit.*
Blount [aside]. Yes; he has no other child! she
must have all his savings; I don't see what harm it

could do me. Still that £10,000, — I want that £10,000: if she would but run off now, one could get rid of the settlements.

Enter STOUT [*wiping his forehead*], *and takes* SIR JOHN *aside.*

Stout. Sir John, we've been played upon! My secretary is brother to Flash's head clerk; Evelyn had not £300 in the bank!

Sir John. Bless us and save us! you take away my breath! But then — Deadly Smooth — the execution — the — oh, he must be done up!

Stout. As to Smooth, he'd "do anything to oblige." All a trick, depend upon it! Smooth has already deceived me, for before the day's over, Evelyn will be member for Groginhole. I've had an express from Popkins; he's in despair! not for *himself* — but for the *country*, Sir John — what's to become of the country?

Sir John. But what could be Evelyn's *object?*

Stout. Object? Do you look for an object in a whimsical creature like that? — a man who has not even any political opinions! Object! Perhaps to break off his match with your daughter! Take care, Sir John, or the borough will be lost to your family!

Sir John. Aha! I begin to smell a rat! But it is not too late yet.

Stout. My interest in Popkins made me run to Lord Spendquick, the late proprietor of Groginhole.

I told him that Evelyn could not pay the rest of the money! and he told me that —

Sir John. What?

Stout. Mr. Sharp had just paid it him; there's no hope for Popkins! England will rue this day!

Sir John. Georgina shall lend him the money! *I'll* lend him — every man in my house shall lend him — I feel again what it is to be a father-in-law!— [*Aside.*] But stop; I'll be cautious. Stout may be on his side — a trap — not likely; but I'll go first to Spendquick myself. Sir Frederick, excuse me — you can't dine with me to-day. And, on second thoughts, I see that it would be very unhandsome to desert poor Evelyn, now he's down in the world. Can't think of it, my dear boy — can't think of it! Very much honoured, and happy to see you as a friend. Waiter, my carriage! Um! What, humbug *Stingy Jack*, will they? Ah! a good joke, indeed! [*Exit.*

Blount. Mr. Stout, what have you been saying to Sir John? Something against my chawacter; I know you have; don't deny it. Sir, I shall expect satisfaction!

Stout. Satisfaction, Sir Frederick? as if a man of enlightenment had any satisfaction in fighting! Did not mention your name; we were talking of Evelyn. Only think! — he's no more ruined than you are.

Blount. Not wuined! Aha, now I understand! So, so! Stay, let me see — she's to meet me in the square!

[*Pulls out his watch; a very small one.*

Stout [pulling out his own: a very large one]. I must be off to the vestry.

Blount. Just in time! — ten thousand pounds! 'Gad, my blood's up, and I won't be tweated in *this* way, if he were fifty times Stingy Jack! [*Exit.*

SCENE II.

The drawing-rooms in SIR JOHN VESEY'S *house.*

LADY FRANKLIN, GRAVES.

Graves. Well, well, I am certain that poor Evelyn loves Clara still, but you can't persuade me that she cares for him.

Lady Frank. She has been breaking her heart ever since she heard of his distress. Nay, I am sure she would give all she has, could it save him from the consequences of his own folly.

Graves [half aside]. She would only give him his own money, if she did. I should like just to sound her.

Lady Frank. [ringing the bell]. And you shall. I take so much interest in her, that I forgive your friend everything but his offer to Georgina.

Enter Servant.

Where are the young ladies?

Ser. Miss Vesey is, I believe, still in the square: Miss Douglas is just come in, my lady.

Lady Frank. What! did she go out with Miss Vesey?

Ser. No, my lady; I attended her to Drummond's the banker. [*Exit.*

Lady Frank. Drummond's!

Enter CLARA.

Why, child, what on earth could take you to Drummond's at this hour of the day?

Clara [*confused*]. Oh, I — that is — I — Ah, Mr. Graves! How is Mr. Evelyn? How does he bear up against so sudden a reverse?

Graves. With an awful calm. I fear all is not right here! [*Touching his head*]. — The report in the town is, that he must go abroad instantly — perhaps to-day.

Clara. Abroad! — to-day!

Graves. But all his creditors will be paid; and he only seems anxious to know if Miss Vesey remains true in his misfortunes.

Clara. Ah? he loves her so *much*, then!

Graves. Um! — That's more than I can say.

Clara. She told me last night, that he said to the last that £10,000 would free him from all his liabilities — that was the sum, was it not?

Graves. Yes; he persists in the same assertion Will Miss Vesey lend it?

Lady Frank. [*aside*]. If she does, I shall not think so well of her poor dear mother; for I am sure she'd be no child of Sir John's!

Graves. I should like to convince myself that my poor friend has nothing to hope from a woman's generosity.

Lady Frank. Civil! And are men, then, less covetous?

Graves. I know one man, at least, who, rejected in his poverty by one as poor as himself, no sooner came into a sudden fortune than he made his lawyer invent a codicil which the testator never dreamt of, bequeathing independence to the woman who had scorned him.

Lady Frank. And never told her?

Graves. Never! There's no such document at Doctors' Commons, depend on it! You seem incredulous, Miss Clara! Good day!

Clara [*following him*]. One word, for mercy's sake! Do I understand you right? Ah, how could I be so blind! Generous Evelyn!

Graves. You appreciate, and *Georgina* will desert him. Miss Douglas, he loves you still. — If that's not just like me! Meddling with other people's affairs, as if they were worth it -- hang them!

[*Exit.*

Clara. Georgina will desert him. Do you think so? — [*Aside.*] Ah, he will soon discover that she never wrote that letter!

Lady Frank. She told me last night that she would never see him again. To do her justice, she's less interested than her father, — and as much attached as she can be to another. Even while engaged to Evelyn, she has met Sir Frederick every day in the square.

Clara. And he is alone — sad — forsaken — ruined. And I, whom he enriched — I, the creature of his bounty — I, once the woman of his love — I stand idly here to content myself with tears and prayers! Oh, Lady Franklin, have pity on me — on him! We are both of kin to him — as relations, we have both a right to comfort! Let us go to him — come!

Lady Frank. No! it would scarcely be right — remember the world — I cannot!

Clara. All abandon him — then I will go alone!

Lady Frank. You! — so proud — so sensitive!

Clara. Pride — when he wants a friend?

Lady Frank. His misfortunes are his own fault — a gambler!

Clara. Can you think of his faults now? *I* have no right to do so. All I have — all — his gift! — and I never to have dreamed it!

Lady Frank. But if Georgina do indeed release him — if she have already done so — what will he think? What but —

Clara. What but — that, if he love me still, I may have enough for both, and I am by his side! But that is too bright a dream. He told me I might call him brother! Where now, should a sister be? But — but — I — I — I — tremble! If, after all — if — if — In one word, am I too bold? The world — my con-

16*

science can answer *that* — but do you think that HE could despise me?

Lady Frank. No, Clara, no! Your fair soul is too transparent for even libertines to misconstrue. Something tells me that this meeting may make the happiness of both! You cannot go alone. My presence justifies all. Give me your hand — we will go together. [*Exeunt.*

SCENE III.

A room in EVELYN'S *house.*

Eve. Yes; as yet, all surpasses my expectations. I am sure of Smooth — I have managed even Sharp; my election will seem but an escape from a prison. Ha! ha! True, it cannot last long; but a few hours more are all I require, and for that time at least I shall hope to be thoroughly ruined.

Enter GRAVES.

Well, Graves, and what do people say of me?

Graves. Everything that's bad!

Eve. Three days ago I was universally respected. I awake this morning to find myself singularly infamous. Yet I'm the same man.

Graves. Humph! why, gambling —

Eve. Cant! it was not criminal to gamble — it was criminal to lose. Tut! — will you deny that if I had ruined Smooth instead of myself, every hand would have grasped mine yet more cordially, and every lip would have smiled congratulation on my success? Man — Man! I've not been rich and poor for nothing! The Vices and the Virtues are written in a language the world cannot construe· it reads them in a vile translation, and the translators are — FAILURE and SUCCESS! You alone are unchanged.

Graves. There's no merit in that. I am always ready to mingle my tears with any man. — [*Aside.*] I know I'm a fool, but I can't help it. Hark ye, Evelyn! I like you — I'm rich; and anything I can do to get you out of your hobble will give me an excuse to grumble for the rest of my life. There, now 'tis out.

Eve. [*touched*]. There's something good in human nature, after all! My dear friend, I will now confide in you: I am not the spendthrift you think me — my losses have been trifling — not a month's income of my fortune, [GRAVES *shakes him heartily by the hand.*] No! — it has been but a stratagem to prove if the love, on which was to rest the happiness of a whole life, were given to the Money or the Man. Now you guess why I have asked from Georgina this one proof of confidence and affection. — Think you she will give it?

Graves. Would you break your heart if she did not?

Eve. It is in vain to deny that I still love Clara; our last conversation renewed feelings which would task all the energies of my soul to conquer. What then? I am not one of those, the Sybarites of sentiment, who deem it impossible for humanity to conquer love — who call their own weakness the voice of a resistless destiny. Such is the poor excuse of every woman who yields her honour — of every adulterer who betrays his friend. No! the heart was given to the soul as its ally, not as its traitor.

Graves. What do you tend to?

Eve. This: — If Georgina still adhere to my fortunes (and I will not put her to too harsh a trial); if she can face the prospect, not of ruin and poverty, but of a moderate independence; if, in one word, she love me for myself, I will shut Clara for ever from my thoughts. I am pledged to Georgina, and I will carry to the altar a soul resolute to deserve her affection and fulfil its vows.

Graves. And if she reject you?

Eve. [*joyfully*]. If she do, I am free once more! And then — then I will dare to ask, for I can ask without dishonour, if Clara can explain the past and bless the future!

Enter Servant *with a letter.*

Eve. [*after reading it*]. The die is cast — the dream is over! Generous girl! Oh, Georgina! I will deserve you yet.

Graves. Georgina! is it possible?

Eve. And the delicacy, the womanhood, the exquisite grace of this! How we misjudge the depth of the human heart! How, seeing the straws on the surface, we forget that the pearls may lie hid below!* I imagined her incapable of this devotion.

Graves. And *I* too.

Eve. It were base in me to continue this trial a moment longer: I will write at once to undeceive that generous heart [*writing*].

Graves. I would have given £ 1,000 if that little jade Clara had been beforehand. But just like my luck: if I want a man to marry one woman, he's sure to marry another on purpose to vex me.

[EVELYN *rings the bell.*

Enter Servant.

Eve. Take this instantly to Miss Vesey; say I will call in an hour. [*Exit* Servant.] And now Clara is resigned for ever! Why does my heart sink within me? Why, why, looking to the fate to come, do I see only the memory of what has been?

Graves. You are re-engaged then to Georgina?

Eve. Irrevocably.

* "Errors like straws," &c.

SCENE IV.

Enter Servant, *announcing* LADY FRANKLIN *and* MISS DOUGLAS.

EVELYN *and* GRAVES.

Lady Frank. My dear Evelyn, you may think it strange to receive such visitors at this moment; but, indeed, it is no time for ceremony. We are your relations — it is reported you are about to leave the country — we come to ask frankly what we can do to serve you?

Eve. Madam — I —

Lady Frank. Come, come — do not hesitate to confide in us; Clara is less a stranger to you than I am: your friend here will perhaps let me consult with him. — [*Aside to* GRAVES.] Let us leave them to themselves.

Graves. You're an angel of a widow; but you come too late, as whatever is good for anything generally does.

[*They retire into the inner room, which should be partially open.*

Eve. Miss Douglas, I may well want words to thank you; this goodness — this sympathy —

Clara [*abandoning herself to her emotion.*] Evelyn! Evelyn! Do not talk thus! — Goodness! sympathy! — I have learned *all* — *all!* It is for ME to speak of gratitude! What! even when I had so wounded you — when you believed me mercenary and cold — when you thought that I was blind and base enough not to know you for what you are; even *at that time* you thought but of my happiness — my fortunes — my fate! — And to you — you — I owe all that has raised the poor orphan from servitude and dependence! While your words were so bitter, your deeds so gentle! Oh, noble Evelyn, this then was your revenge!

Eve. You owe me no thanks — that revenge was sweet! Think you it was nothing to feel that my presence haunted you, though you knew it not? — that in things the pettiest as the greatest, which that gold could buy — the very jewels you wore — the very robe in which, to other eyes, you might seem more fair — in all in which you took the woman's young and innocent delight — *I* had a part — a share? that, even if separated for ever — even if another's — even in distant years — perhaps in a happy home, listening to sweet voices that might call you "mother!" — even then should the uses of that dross bring to your lips one smile — that smile was mine — due to me — due, as a sacred debt, to the hand that you rejected — to the love that you despised!

Clara. Despised! See the proof that I despise you! — see: in this hour, when they say you are again as poor as before, I forget the world — my pride — perhaps too much my sex: I remember but your sorrows — I am here!

Eve. [*aside.*] Oh, Heaven! give me strength to bear

it! — [*Aloud.*] And is this the same voice that, when I knelt at your feet — when I asked but *one day* the hope to call you mine — spoke only of poverty, and answered, "*Never*"?

Clara. Because I had been unworthy of your love if I had insured your misery. Evelyn, hear me! My father, like you, was poor — generous; gifted, like you, with genius — ambition: sensitive, like you, to the least breath of insult. He married, as you would have done — married one whose only dower was penury and care! Alfred, I saw that genius the curse to itself! I saw that ambition wither to despair! — I saw the struggle — the humiliation — the proud man's agony — the bitter life — the early death! — and heard over his breathless clay my mother's groan of self-reproach! Alfred Evelyn, now speak! Was the woman you loved so nobly to repay you with such a doom?

Eve. Clara, we should have shared it!

Clara. Shared? Never let the woman who really loves, comfort her selfishness with such delusion! In marriages like this, the wife cannot share the burden; it is he — the husband — to provide, to scheme, to work, to endure — to grind out his strong heart at the miserable wheel! The wife, alas! cannot share the struggle — she can but witness the despair! And therefore, Alfred, I rejected you.

Eve. Yet you believe me as poor now as I was then.

Clara. But *I* am not poor: *we* are not so poor Of this fortune, which is all your own — if, as I hear, one half would free you from your debts, why, we have the other half still left. Evelyn! it is humble — but it is not penury.

Eve. Cease, cease — you know not how you torture me. Oh, that when hope was possible; — oh, that you had bid me take it to my breast and wait for a brighter day!

Clara. And so have consumed your life of life upon a hope perhaps delayed till age — shut you from a happier choice, from fairer fortunes — shackled you with vows that, as my youth and its poor attributes decayed, would only have irritated and galled — made your whole existence one long suspense! No, Alfred, even *yet* you do not know me!

Eve. Know you! Fair angel, too excellent for man's harder nature to understand! — at least it is permitted me to revere. Why were such blessed words not vouchsafed to me before? — why, why come they now? — too late! Oh, Heaven — too late!

Clara. Too late! What, then, have I said?

Eve. Wealth! what is it without you? *With* you, I recognize its power; to forestall your every wish — to smooth your every path — to make all that life borrows from Grace and Beauty your ministrant and hand maid; and then, looking to those eyes, to read there the treasures of a heart that excelled all that kings could lavish; — why *that* were to make gold indeed a god! But vain — vain — vain! Bound by every tie of faith, gratitude, loyalty, and honour, to another!

Clara. Another! Is she, then, true to your reverses? I did not know this — indeed I did not! And I have thus betrayed myself! O, shame! he must despise me now!

SCENE V.

The foregoing. — *Enter* Sir John; *at the same time* Graves *and* Lady Franklin *advance from the inner room.*

Sir John [*with dignity and frankness*]. Evelyn, I was hasty yesterday. You must own it natural that I should be so. But Georgina has been so urgent in your defence, that — [*as* Lady Franklin *comes up to listen*] Sister, just shut the door, will you — that I cannot resist her. What's money without happiness? So give me your security; for she insists on lending you the £10,000.

Eve. I know, and have already received it.

Sir John. Already received it! Is he joking? Faith, for the last two days I believe I have been living amongst the Mysteries of Udolpho! Sister, have you seen Georgina?

Lady Frank. Not since she went out to walk in the square.

Sir John [*aside*]. She's not in the square nor the house — where the deuce can the girl be?

Eve. I have written to Miss Vesey — I have asked her to fix the day for our wedding.

Sir John [*joyfully*]. Have you? Go, Lady Franklin, find her instantly — she must be back by this time: take my carriage, it is but a step — you will not be two minutes gone. — [*Aside*]. I'd go myself, but I'm afraid of leaving him a moment while he's in such excellent dispositions.

Lady Frank. [*repulsing* CLARA]. No, no: stay till I return. [*Exit.*

Sir John. And don't be down-hearted, my dear fellow; if the worst come to the worst, you will have everything I can leave you. Meantime, if I can in any way help you —

Eve. Ha! — you! — you, too? — Sir John, you have seen my letter to Miss Vesey? — [*Aside*] — or could she have learned the truth before she ventured to be generous?

Sir John. No! on my honour. I only just called at the door on my way from Lord Spend — that is, from the City. Georgina was out; — was ever anything so unlucky? — [*Without.*] [Hurrah — hurrah! Blue for ever!] — What's that?

Enter SHARP.

Sharp. Sir, a deputation from Groginhole — poll closed in the first hour — you are returned! Holloa, sir — holloa!

Eve. And it was to please Clara!

Sir John. Mr. Sharp — Mr. Sharp — I say, how much has Mr. Evelyn lost by Messrs. Flash and Co?

Sharp. Oh, a great deal, sir, — a great deal.

Sir John. [*alarmed*]. How? — a great deal!

Eve. Speak the truth, Sharp, — concealment is all over.

Sharp. £223. 6 s. 3 d. — a great sum to throw away!

Graves. Ah, I comprehend now! Poor Evelyn caught in his own trap!

Sir John. Eh! what, my dear boy? — what? Ha! ha! all humbug, was it? — all humbug, upon my soul! So, Mr. Sharp, isn't he ruined after all? — not the least, wee, rascally, little bit in the world, ruined?

Sharp. Sir, he has never even lived up to his income.

Sir John. Worthy man! I could jump up to the ceiling! I am the happiest father-in-law in the three kingdoms. — And that's my sister's knock, too.

Clara. Since I was mistaken, cousin, — since, now, you do not need me, — forget what has passed: my business here is over. Farewell!

Eve. Could you but see my heart at this moment, with what love, what veneration, what anguish it is filled, you would know how little, in the great calamities of life, fortune is really worth. And must we part now, — *now*, when — when — I never wept before, since my mother died!

Enter LADY FRANKLIN *and* GEORGINA, *followed by* BLOUNT, *who looks shy and embarrassed.*

Graves. Georgina herself — then there's no hope.

Sir John. What the deuce brings that fellow Blount here? — Georgy, my dear Georgy, I want to —

Eve. Stand back, Sir John!

Sir John. But I must speak a word to her — I want to —

Eve. Stand back, I say, — not a whisper — not a sign. If your daughter is to be my wife, to *her* heart only will I look for a reply to *mine.*

Lady Frank. [*to* GEORGINA]. Speak the truth, niece.

Eve. Georgina, it is true, then, that you trust me with your confidence — your fortune? It is also true, that when you did so you believed me ruined? Oh, pardon the doubt! Answer as if your father stood not there — answer me from that truth the world cannot yet have plucked from your soul — answer as if the woe or weal of a life trembled in the balance — answer as the woman's heart, yet virgin and unpolluted, *should* answer to one who has trusted to it his all!

Geor. What can he mean?

Sir John [*making signs*]. She'll not look this way, she will not — hang her — HEM!

Eve. You falter. I implore — I adjure you — answer!

Lady Frank. The truth!

Geor. Mr. Evelyn, your fortune might well dazzle me, as it dazzled others. Believe me, I sincerely pity your reverses.

Sir John. Good girl! you hear her, Evelyn.

Geor. What's money without happiness?

Sir John. Clever creature! — my own sentiments!

Geor. And so, as our engagement is now annulled, — papa told me so this very morning, — I have promised my hand where I have given my heart — to Sir Frederick Blount.

Sir John. I told you, — I? No such thing — no such thing: you frighten her out of her wits — she don't know what she's saying.

Eve. Am I awake? But this letter — this letter, received to-day —

Lady Frank. [*looking over the letter*]. Drummond's — from a banker!

Eve. Read — read.

Lady Frank. "Ten thousand pounds just placed to your account — from the same unknown friend to Evelyn." Oh, Clara, I know now why you went to Drummond's this morning.

Eve. Clara! What! — and the former one with the same signature, on the faith of which I pledged my hand and sacrificed my heart —

Lady Frank. Was written under my eyes, and the secret kept that —

Eve. Look up, look up, Clara — I am free! — I am released! you forgive me? — you love me? — you are mine! We are rich — rich! I can give you fortune, power, — I can devote to you my whole life, thought, heart, soul — I am all yours, Clara — my own — my wife!

Sir John. [*to* GEORGINA]. So, you've lost the game by a revoke, in trumping your own father's best of a suit! — Unnatural jade! — Aha, Lady Franklin — I am to thank you for this!

Lady Frank. You've to thank me that she's not now on the road to Scotland with Sir Frederick. I chanced on them by the Park just in time to dissuade and save her. But, to do her justice, a hint of your displeasure was sufficient.

Geor. [*half-sobbing*]. And you know, papa, you said this very morning that poor Frederick had been very ill-used and you would settle it all at the club.

Blount. Come, Sir John, you can only blame yourself and Evelyn's cunning device. After all, I'm no such vewy bad match; and as for the £10,000 —

Eve. I'll double it. Ah, Sir John, what's money without happiness?

Sir John. Pshaw — nonsense — stuff! Don't humbug me!

Lady Frank. But if you don't consent, she'll have no husband at all.

Sir John. Hum! there's something in that. [*Aside to* EVELYN.] Double it, will you? Then settle it all *tightly* on her. Well — well — my foible is not avarice. Blount, make her happy. Child, I forgive you. — [*Pinching her arm.*] Ugh, you fool!

Graves [*to* LADY FRANKLIN]. I'm afraid it's catching. What say you? I feel the symptoms of matrimony creeping all over me. Shall we, eh? Frankly, now, frankly —

Lady Frank. Frankly, now, there's my hand, on

one condition, — that we finish our reel on the wedding-day.

Graves. Accepted. Is it possible? Sainted Maria! thank Heaven you are spared this affliction!

Enter SMOOTH.

Smooth. How d'ye do, Alfred? I intrude, I fear! Quite a family party.

Blount. Wish us joy, Smooth — Georgina's mine, and —

Smooth. And our four friends there apparently have made up another rubber. John, my dear boy, you look as if you had something at stake on the odd trick.

Sir John. Sir, your very — Confound the fellow! and he's a dead shot, too!

Enter STOUT *and* GLOSSMORE *hastily, talking with each other.*

Stout. I'm sure he's of our side; we've all the intelligence.

Gloss. I'm sure he's of our's if his fortune is safe, for we've all the property. — My dear Evelyn, you were out of humour yesterday — but I forgive you.

Stout. Certainly! — what would become of public life if a man were obliged to be two days running in the same mind? — I rise to explain. — Just heard of your return, Evelyn. Congratulate you. The great motion of the session is fixed for Friday. We count on your vote. Progress with the times!

Gloss. Preserve the Constitution!

Stout. Your money will do wonders for the party! — Advance!

Gloss. The party respects men of your property!— Stick fast!

Eve. I have the greatest respect, I assure you, for the worthy and intelligent flies upon both sides the wheel; but whether we go too fast or too slow, does not, I fancy, depend so much on the flies as on the Stout Gentleman who sits inside and pays the post-boys. Now all my politics as yet is to consider what's best for the Stout Gentleman!

Smooth. Meaning John Bull. *Ce cher* old John!

Stout. I'm as wise as I was before.

Gloss. Sir, he's a trimmer!

Eve. Smooth, we have yet to settle our first piquet account and our last! And I sincerely thank you for the service you have rendered to me, and the lesson you have given these gentlemen. — [*Turning to* CLARA.] Ah, Clara, you — you have succeeded where wealth had failed! You have reconciled me to the world and to mankind. My friends — we must confess it — amidst the humours and the follies, the vanities, deceits, and vices that play their parts in the great Comedy of Life — it is our own fault if we do not find such natures, though rare and few, as redeem the rest, brightening the shadows that are flung from the form and body of the TIME with glimpses of the everlasting holiness of truth and love.

Graves. But for the truth and the love, when found, to make us tolerably happy, we should not be without —

Lady Frank. Good health;
Graves. Good spirits;
Clara. A good heart;
Smooth. An innocent rubber;
Geor. Congenial tempers;
Blount. A pwoper degwee of pwudence;
Stout. Enlightened opinions;
Gloss. Constitutional principles;
Sir John. Knowledge of the world;
Eve. And — plenty of Money!

END OF VOL. I.

www.ingramcontent.com/pod-product-compliance
Lightning Source LLC
Chambersburg PA
CBHW032145230426
43672CB00011B/2459